# JUNIOR HIGH SCHOOL COSTS

By
Wilbur I. Gooch, Ph. D.

TEACHERS COLLEGE, COLUMBIA UNIVERSITY

CONTRIBUTIONS TO EDUCATION, NO. 604

Published with the approval of
*Professor* JOHN K. NORTON, *Sponsor*

BUREAU OF PUBLICATIONS
Teachers College, Columbia University
NEW YORK CITY
1934

Cop. 1

PRINTED IN THE UNITED STATES OF AMERICA
AT THE COUNTRY LIFE PRESS
GARDEN CITY, NEW YORK

# Acknowledgments

THE author is grateful to Professor Paul R. Mort for the opportunity to pursue this study, and to Professor Carter Alexander and Professor Edwin H. Reeder, advisers, for their continued advice and assistance. He is particularly indebted to Professor John K. Norton, sponsor, who from the inception of the study to its close was a source of stimulating guidance and encouragement.

Professor George D. Strayer and Professor N. L. Engelhardt gave valuable advice both in seminar and in personal conference.

Miss Eliza Tarrant rendered important service in reducing much of the raw data to usable form and in revising the manuscript.

W. I. G.

# Contents

# Tables

# Tables

# JUNIOR HIGH SCHOOL COSTS

# I

# Previous Studies

WHEN school officials consider replacing the traditional 8–4 plan of educational structure with the junior high school type of organization, they usually study the problem from two angles—first, the educational significance of the change, and second, the financial implications. And, while educational policy should not be determined solely from the standpoint of expense, circumstances require that boards of education and superintendents of schools give particular attention to these financial implications.

There is a rather prevalent opinion among authorities in the junior high school field and among educators in general that the establishment of the junior high school introduces new and increased financial obligations. This common opinion is based upon certain a priori considerations and upon a number of investigations which have advanced important statistical data. A review of these investigations reveals what is at present available in the way of factual material in the field of junior high school costs and at the same time reveals the need of further examination of the problem.

The first attempt to investigate and report junior high school costs in any extensive or comprehensive way was made by Childs.[1] In 1918 he published a study which was made to ascertain the nature and extent of the reorganization movement in Indiana and to "measure specifically certain claimed advantages or objections to junior high school organization." In connection with the last named purpose Childs included the item of cost because he noted that "one of the chief objections that has been advanced against the reorganization movement has been its greater cost" and because "at the present time common opinion seems to take higher costs for granted in the junior high school than in the traditional grammar grades."

Childs's method of investigation was to send out "inquiry forms"

---

[1] H. G. Childs, *An Investigation of Certain Phases of the Reorganization Movement in the Grammar Grades of Indiana Public Schools*, Fort Wayne Printing Co., Fort Wayne, Indiana, 1918.

1

requesting the total annual salaries paid teachers, principals, and supervisors in three groups of grades—1 to 6, 7 and 8, and 9 to 12. This questionnaire was sent to three types of organizations—junior high schools, departmental schools, and non-departmental schools. When the results were tabulated it was found that in the three types of organizations per pupil costs in grades 1 to 6 presented but slight variations. Likewise, in grades 9 to 12 the variations were not marked. However, grades 7 and 8 in the junior high school group carried an average (median) per pupil cost approximately 33 per cent higher than that of the two other groups. When the results were tabulated on the basis of population, it was found that in systems in cities of more than 5,000 population junior high school grades 7 and 8 carried a per pupil cost only 6 per cent higher than that of grades 7 and 8 in the departmental group. In the schools located in communities of less than 5,000 population, however, junior high school grades 7 and 8 showed a per pupil cost 50.8 per cent higher than in the departmental group. The investigator did not believe, however, that these figures could "be taken at their face value in ascertaining the real cost conditions, but rather there should be an investigation of the costs covering the entire six upper grades in both groups of schools." Resorting to comparison on that basis Childs finally reached the conclusion that "from the foregoing analysis it appears that in both the larger city and the smaller consolidated schools, considered separately, the junior-senior high school cost does not exceed the 8–4 plan for the upper six grades by more than 6 per cent. For village and small city junior high schools the per capita cost for the upper six grades is approximately 15 per cent to 20 per cent more than for departmental schools."

An application of Childs's study at the present time requires that several factors be given careful attention. It was an investigation of one state only, undertaken in 1918, a time so far distant as to make almost certain major changes in many aspects of the problem. At that time thirty-five Indiana public schools claimed junior high school organization, but twenty-five of these had been reorganized in 1915 or later and hence for so short a period that there is little assurance that their costs were representative of the junior high school type of organization. The schools included in the investigation seemingly were not clear-cut types but might be classed to-day as 6–2–4, 6–6, and 6–3–3, the majority of them belonging to the 6–2–4 and 6–6 groups. The investigation is limited to the cost of instruction for salaries of teachers, principals, and supervisors. Finally, the investigator relied on a direct comparison of costs. That is, because grades 7 and 8 in junior high schools showed a median cost of $27.55 per pupil and grades 7 and 8 in departmental schools showed a median per pupil cost of $25.90, it is stated that grades 7 and 8 in the junior high school type of organization show a per pupil cost $1.65, or 6 per cent, higher than grades 7 and 8 in departmental schools. No one may question this statement. But one might question the conclusion that this difference is due to type of organization. That is, many factors other than type of organization may have determined that costs were 6 per cent higher for the junior high schools than for departmental schools.[2]

Briggs[3] in his volume on the junior high school published in 1920 included a chapter on costs. After commenting on the exceeding complexity of educational costs, Briggs introduced the results of a questionnaire study. An attempt was made to secure the per pupil costs for instruction and maintenance in grades 1 to 6, 1 to 8, 7 and 8, the junior high school, and the senior high school in a number of school systems located in various sections of the country. The questionnaire was sent only to school systems having the junior high school type of organization. Hence, no attempt was made by Briggs to compare a junior high school group with a non-junior high school group as was done by Childs. Instead, the comparison was made within the group of junior high school systems; that is, the cost of the junior high school grades was compared with the cost of the elementary and senior high school grades. This eliminated entirely the questionable procedure of making a direct comparison of per pupil costs in a group of junior high school systems with the per pupil costs in a group of non-junior high school systems.

[2] It is true that Childs reported the per pupil costs for grades 1 to 6 and grades 9 to 12 in order that one might draw one's own conclusions as to the comparability of the two groups. This was an excellent safeguard, but its value is considerably lessened by the fact that grades 1 to 6, 7 and 8, and 9 to 12 do not constitute corresponding groups. That is, in several cases costs are reported for certain schools for grades 1 to 6 but not for grades 7 and 8, in other cases for grades 9 to 12 but not for grades 7 and 8, and in still other cases for grades 7 and 8 but not for grades 1 to 6 or for grades 9 to 12. If every school had reported cost data for each group of grades the results might have been considerably different, particularly since so few schools were included in the investigation. It is especially noticeable that those two schools which reported the highest junior high school costs do not carry a report of the costs of grades 1 to 6 or grades 9 to 12.

[3] T. H. Briggs, *The Junior High School*, Chapter XII, Houghton Mifflin Company, 1920.

After eliminating cities making incomplete returns, Briggs had a total of twenty-two systems reporting costs for the first six grades, the junior high school, and the senior high school. Hence, unlike the situation reported by Childs the twenty-two junior high schools used in this investigation were in the same school systems as the twenty-two elementary and senior high schools.

Briggs found that for the twenty-two cities, representing fourteen states from Connecticut to California, the average per pupil costs for instruction and maintenance were $31.38 for grades 1 to 6, $50.04 for the junior high school grades, and $63.48 for the senior high school grades. These figures definitely established the cost position of the junior high school in relation to the two other grade divisions for these twenty-two school systems and gave an indication of what might be expected in other junior high school systems.

Having related the cost of the junior high school unit to the cost of the grades below and above it, Briggs then attempted "to compare the cost of systems with and without junior high schools." In order to accomplish this with the data which he had at hand he used a procedure which he described as follows:

If we assume that the pupils in these twenty-two cities are distributed through the grades according to the estimate of the United States Commissioner of Education for the country at large, and if we assume, further, that without junior high schools the per capita cost for the first six grades would remain the same through grades seven and eight, and that the per capita cost for the senior high schools would be the same with the ninth grade included, then we are able to compare the cost of systems with and without junior high schools.

Briggs did not attempt to build up a case for these assumptions; he merely indicated that in so far as they were correct his findings were correct. He referred to the result obtained by this procedure as an "estimate."

In addition to his questionnaire study Briggs reported a considerable number of individual city investigations which in some instances took the form of an estimate rather than a systematic inquiry into costs. These investigations included those of the St. Louis school authorities in the Ben Blewett Junior High School of that city; C. O. Davis in Grand Rapids, Michigan; C. O. Davis and J. A. Starkweather in Kalamazoo, Michigan; F. P. Bachman in New York City; George Wheeler in Philadelphia; O. C. Barker in Oakland, California; and F. V. Thompson in Boston. Each of these inquiries into the cost of junior high school education is of value for the place and time conducted. However, the great period of junior high school reorganization has come since the time of the above reports and it is doubtful if the findings indicated by these studies would be representative of the situation to-day.

One of the more recent investigations of the cost of junior high school education is that reported by the Department of Superintendence in the *Fifth Yearbook*.[4] This, like those of Childs and Briggs, was made by means of a questionnaire. Inquiries were sent out in the fall of 1926 to all cities of more than 30,000 population which had adopted, at least in part, the junior high school type of organization. The results were tabulated in two groups, those of more than 100,000 population and those of less than 100,000. Thirteen cities are included in the former group and thirty-three in the latter. In the larger cities the per pupil cost for current expenses in the junior high school exceeds that of the elementary school by 39 per cent and in the smaller cities by 44 per cent. In the larger cities senior high school costs are reported as 78 per cent above elementary school costs and in the smaller cities as 89 per cent above elementary school costs. It will be noted that junior high school costs for both groups of cities fall almost exactly midway between elementary school costs and senior high school costs.

Here, as in Briggs's investigation, there is a definite placing of the cost position of the junior high school unit in relation to the elementary and senior high school units. And the assumption was made, as it was by Briggs, that since the junior high school unit consistently shows a higher cost than grades 1 to 6 in junior high school systems, the junior high school unit will likewise show a higher cost than grades 1 to 8 in non-junior high school systems. However, after making the statement that "the adoption of the 6–3–3 plan of organization means an increase in the cost per pupil for children in seventh and eighth grades" (this statement is based on the fact that grades 7 to 9 show a higher cost than grades 1 to 6 in 6–3–3 systems), the investigation proceeds with caution to point out that the adoption of the 6–3–3 plan also means "a decrease in the cost for those in the ninth grade." Likewise, it is indicated that "there is the further consideration that the seventh and eighth grades under the traditional plan usually cost something

[4]National Education Association, Department of Superintendence, *Fifth Yearbook*, "The Junior High School Curriculum," Chapter VI, 1927.

more per pupil than the lower grades." The Yearbook then points out that "these factors might lead one to conclude that Tables 19 and 20 [these tables report the relative costs of grades 1 to 6, 7 to 9, and 10 to 12 for the two population groups] tend to exaggerate the increase in cost likely to result from adoption of the junior high school unit."

Koos[5] in his enlarged edition on the junior high school, published in 1927, devotes little space to the question of costs. His position, however, is quite definite when he states that

> It should be clear on a priori grounds that to provide satisfactory junior-high-school education, with all that this implies in elective curricula, better-trained teachers, expensive plant, and adequate equipment, must cost more than to provide the kind of training characteristic of the upper elementary grades, since all items of cost involved will tend to approach those of the traditional high school.

Koos also introduces some "statistical evidence that the junior high school is more expensive than the grade organization." He draws from the Grand Rapids, Michigan, School Survey to show that "segregation of the upper grades in the so-called intermediate school means a very considerable addition to the cost of instruction." Likewise, he points out that Childs found this to be true in Indiana. Finally, he introduces evidence from Morrison's *The Financing of Public Schools in the State of Illinois.*[6] From this evidence Koos, in common with others, apparently assumes that because Morrison found costs to be higher in grades 7 to 9 than in grades 1 to 6 in junior high school systems, costs in grades 7 to 9 in junior high school systems would be higher than costs in grades 7 to 9 in 8–4 systems.

Assistant Superintendent Gould of Los Angeles in his contribution to Proctor and Ricciardi's volume[7] on the junior high school uses the experience of Los Angeles to show that the junior high school involves added expenditures. He states that "for the year 1927–28 the total cost per unit of average daily attendance in junior high schools [of Los Angeles], including all items of current expense, was $136.35. As against this, the elementary schools for the same year showed a total cost per pupil of $99.88." Here again

[5]L. V. Koos, *The Junior High School*, pp. 106–108, Enlarged Edition, Ginn and Company, 1927.

[6]H. C. Morrison, *The Financing of Public Schools in the State of Illinois*, Educational Financia Inquiry Commission, Vol. 9, The Macmillan Company, 1924.

[7]W. M. Proctor and N. Ricciardi, *The Junior High School, Its Organization and Administration*, pp. 261–262, Stanford University Press, 1930.

is seen the tendency to measure the cost of the junior high school
by comparing it with the cost of the elementary grades of the same
system.   However, Gould, indicating that this type of cost meas-
urement probably does not involve all the factors in the situation,
continues,"It must be remembered that in most of these elementary
schools there were no seventh and eighth grades . . . and that
if the ninth-grade pupils were not being carried in a junior high
school at the unit cost which prevails there they would have to be
carried in a four-year high school at a much higher unit cost.
Quoting again from the Los Angeles situation, the unit cost in the
high schools for the year 1927–1928 was $174.72, as against the
$136.35 per unit of average daily attendance for junior high
schools."  There is then the feeling that the per pupil costs in
grades 1 to 6 might not average the same as in grades 1 to 8.   Likewise, there is introduced the factor of the effect of the presence of
the ninth grade.   This writer indicates that if the ninth grade
pupils were not being carried in a junior high school they would
have to be carried in a four-year high school "at a much higher
unit cost."   But how may the cost effect of the ninth grade be
measured?   In terms of the difference in per pupil costs between
the junior high school unit and the senior high school unit?   Such a
procedure seems valid but it assumes an equal distribution of costs
for grades 9 to 12 in the traditional high school.

   Davis,[8] writing in 1925, states that "all the statistics available
tend to show that while the junior high school, as a rule, costs somewhat more than the elementary schools in the same system, it costs
less than the senior high school.   Hence what is added in one place
is subtracted in another.   Moreover, if a community sows sparingly, it must expect to reap sparingly.   The junior high school
costs very little more than the traditional type of school, and it is
worth whatever it costs."   Apparently Davis believes that since
the statistics show a somewhat higher cost in the junior high school
unit than in the elementary unit of the same system the junior
high school costs more than the traditional school.   Moreover,
he believes that since the senior high school unit shows a higher cost
than the junior high school unit the presence of the ninth grade in
the junior high school unit will "subtract," at least in part, the
expense which is added by a higher cost for grades 7 and 8.   But
how may the added costs of grades 7 and 8 and the subtracted

[8]C. O. Davis, *Junior High School Education*, p. 351, World Book Company, 1924.

costs of grade 9 be measured?    Evidently it has been assumed that
if the system were a traditional 8–4 type instead of a junior high
school type, costs in grades 7 and 8 would be the same as costs in
grades 1 to 6, and that costs in grade 9 would be the same as costs
in grades 10 to 12.

In his treatise on high school administration Foster[9] states that
"in general, the consensus of opinion is that in cost the junior high
school ranks between the senior high school or four-year high school
and the elementary school."    This statement is borne out by past
investigations.    However, there seems to be in the statement an
indication of the same prevalent tendency to think of the senior
high school unit of grades 10 to 12 as comparable to the high school
unit of grades 9 to 12, and to think of the elementary unit of grades
1 to 6 in the junior high school system as comparable to the elementary unit of grades 1 to 8 in the traditional system.

A number of other investigations have been made.[10]    In general
they reach conclusions, or infer conclusions, similar to those
reported above.    An opinion, such as that of Superintendent
Thompson of Boston quoted by Briggs, is occasionally reported to
the effect that the junior high school will reduce costs.    But the
practically unanimous opinion of those who have carefully investigated the matter is that the junior high school, since it offers a
superior type of educational program, must inevitably cost more.

But what is meant by the statement that "the junior high school
costs more?"    Does it mean that a school system organized on
some junior high school basis will cost more as a whole than this
same school system would cost if organized on the traditional or
8–4 basis?    Or does it mean that the grades involved in the junior
high school unit (as grades 7 to 9 in a 6–3–3 system) will cost more
than would these same grades if organized on the 8–4 basis?    Or
does it mean that the grades of the junior high school unit will cost

[9]H. H. Foster, *High School Administration*, p. 474, The Century Co., 1928.

[10]In addition to a great number of individual school investigations made during the early part of the
reorganization movement, the majority of which are reported by Childs and Briggs, a number of later
investigations have been made dealing with particular phases of the cost of junior high school education such as:

Cleveland, Ohio, Bureau of Statistics and Child Accounting, *The Expenditures for Teachers' Salaries
Distributed on a Subject Taught Basis, Cleveland Junior High Schools, 1928–1929.*  Cleveland, Ohio,
Board of Education, 1929.

A. R. Joyal, *The Cost of Instruction in California Junior High Schools.*  M. A. Thesis, 1926, University of California, Berkeley, California.

D. H. Pierce, *Teaching Costs in Thirty-Nine Junior High Schools*, United States Bureau of Education,
Leaflet No. 16, 1924.

more than would grades 1 to 8 if the system were organized on the 8–4 basis? Or does it mean that the junior high school unit will cost more than the elementary unit of the same system? Childs attacked the problem by asking: Do grades 7 and 8 in a junior high school cost more than grades 7 and 8 in an unreorganized school? To answer this question he compared directly per pupil costs in grades 7 and 8 in the junior high school type of organization with costs in these grades in the traditional type. Briggs's method of approach was primarily to relate costs in the junior high school unit to costs in the two other units of the same system. Then from the data thus secured he proceeded to answer the question, does the junior high school type of organization cost more than the traditional type? The investigation reported by the *Fifth Yearbook* of the Department of Superintendence bases its conclusions on the same initial procedure as that of Briggs. If one continues through the list of investigations and opinions, one will find that the statement that the junior high school costs more means a variety of things and that it has been made to comprehend any one or several phases of the problems which are included in the questions indicated above. Moreover, one will often find either that there is little or no attempt to distinguish between these different questions, or that it is implied or assumed that in reality these questions resolve themselves into one and the answer to all is included in the answer to any one.

A careful scrutiny of the past investigations with respect to the time that they were made, the questions they sought to answer, and the methods of gaining answers to their questions leads to the following conclusions, some of which indicate where further study might prove of value in the field of junior high school costs.

First, many of the more important studies were undertaken at a time when junior high school cost data were less available and less reliable than they are to-day. They were less reliable partly because financial records on the whole were less accurate than at present but chiefly because the junior high schools of fifteen and twenty years ago were transitional or experimental in nature and presented a much less stable situation than they do to-day.

Second, in the majority of investigations the procedure consisted in securing per pupil costs in grades 1 to 6, 7 to 9, and 10 to 12 in junior high school organizations only. Then it was assumed that without junior high schools (that is, in traditional organizations) per pupil costs in grades 1 to 6 would remain the same through grades 7 and 8. From this it was concluded that per pupil costs in grades 7 and 8 are higher in the junior high school type of organization.

Third, in many cases, particularly those investigations of individual schools, only grades 7 and 8 were included in the study, the effect of grade 9 being completely ignored.

Fourth, there has been no consistent attempt to differentiate between types of junior high schools. The majority of investigations have included indiscriminately 6–2–4, 6–3–3, and 6–6 types.

Fifth, cost investigations generally have failed to make any differentiations between the various characteristics or features of the junior high school. Hence, it is not known to what extent the costs that have been reported are inherent in the type of organization, which involves the regrouping of grades, and to what extent they are to be associated with the reorganized program of education, which involves certain features of progressive education.[11]

[11]While the junior high school is more than a regrouping of grades it may be looked upon as a type of organization in which certain grades are segregated from either or both of the customary 8–4 units, plus a program of education which involves certain features of progressive education. (See Chapter IX.)

# II
# The Problem

Past investigations in one way or another have sought to discover the financial consequences of shifting a school system from the traditional type of organization to the junior high school type. The primary purpose of this study does not differ greatly from the purposes of other studies in the field. It seeks to answer this question: What are the factors affecting the cost of education in the junior high school type of organization as distinguished from the traditional type? It seeks, moreover, to answer this question without recourse to certain assumptions hitherto made, and by relating variations in cost more specifically than has hitherto been done to the factors which apparently determine these variations.

It has been found advisable to limit the scope of the problem rather sharply in several ways as indicated below.

## TYPE OF ORGANIZATION

Although the 6–3–3 type of organization is generally recognized as the junior high school, several other methods of grade grouping have been widely used. Koos[1] reports several investigations in which the data show that the 6–2–4 plan is the one most common in practice, but he also reports others which indicate that the 6–3–3 plan is most widely used. He believes that "inferences from the results of such inquiries may properly be that smaller cities and reorganizations more recently effected show larger proportions of two-year units, and larger cities and more thoroughly established reorganizations show larger proportions of three-year units."

The Department of Superintendence of the National Education Association in its *Fifth Yearbook*[2] presents evidence that over 75 per cent of the separately organized junior high schools include grades 7 to 9. However, further evidence shows that at the time

[1]L. V. Koos, *The Junior High School*, pp. 132–138, Ginn and Company, 1927.
[2]National Education Association, Department of Superintendence, *Fifth Yearbook*, p. 26.

these data were collected there were nearly twice as many junior-senior systems as segregated systems and that the former were about evenly divided between the 7, 8–9, 10, 11, 12 type and the 7, 8, 9–10, 11, 12 type.[3]   If separately organized these would correspond to the 6–2–4 and 6–3–3 types, respectively.   The 6–6 plan seems to have made its greatest growth in the smaller communities of Indiana, Iowa, Michigan, Ohio, Oklahoma, and Pennsylvania.

Proctor and Ricciardi[4] in a survey of the 152 junior high schools listed in the Directory of California Secondary Schools, published in 1930, found that one school included grade 7; three included grades 7 and 8; 139 included grades 7, 8, and 9; and nine included grades 7, 8, 9, and 10.

The Biennial Survey of Education in the United States, 1928–1930,[5] lists a total of 1,566 segregated junior high schools of which 1,118 included grades 7, 8, and 9.   One thousand four hundred and eighty are reported as junior-senior high schools with the majority (829) organized as 7–9, 10–12 systems.   One thousand two hundred and one are reported as undivided reorganized high schools of which the overwhelming majority (925) are 7–12 schools.   Other data are reported giving reorganization status and reorganization plans for 157 cities of more than 30,000 population in which it is shown that development is toward the 6–3–3 plan in 107 of these cities.

It will be noted that the reorganization movement has taken on some complex aspects due to the fact that it has resulted in three general types of schools, segregated junior high schools, junior-senior high schools, and undivided reorganized high schools, and that *each* of these types has various plans of grade grouping.   This has resulted in at least 25 different combinations being reported as making some claim to junior high school organization.   In addition to this it is found that the junior college movement has added certain other possible grade groupings as 6–3–3–2, 6–4–4, 6–4–2–2.   Out of this complex situation two developments seem outstanding: (1) the school systems of the larger cities are extensively committed to the 6–3–3 type of organization, sometimes with the addition of a junior college; (2) the reorganization movement is finding its way into smaller school systems in the form of

[3]National Education Association, Department of Superintendence, *Fifth Yearbook*, Table 4, pp. 28–29.
[4]W. M. Proctor and N. Ricciardi, *The Junior High School*, p. 1, Stanford University Press, 1930.
[5]*Biennial Survey of Education, 1928–1930*, United States Office of Education, Bulletin (1931) No. 20; Vol. I, Chapter III, Table 2, pp. 124 and 125.

the undivided school which as to grade grouping is predominantly the 7–12 type.

In the opinion of the United States Office of Education "the tendency is toward a general acceptance of the K 6–3–3 plan of organization but this and the K 6–6 plan and the addition of two years of junior college tend to be modified according to local needs and ideals."[6]

A considerable body of authoritative opinion[7] is in favor of the 6–3–3 type of organization for cities where total enrollment is sufficiently large to have an effective organization and where economy will not be sacrificed because of smaller units of organization as opposed to larger units. Because both present practice and considerable weight of opinion incline toward the 6–3–3 plan[8] and because one study cannot well comprehend all types of organizations with their many possible cost issues and ramifications, this present study is limited to the 6–3–3 type of organization.

## SIZE OF SCHOOL

This study is further limited to include only school systems of cities which have a total population of 5,000 or more. This size limit was set not because of any evidence or opinion that the 6–3–3 type of organization is not suited to school systems of somewhat smaller cities, but because it was believed that an effective 6–3–3 organization could be established in a community of this size

---

[6]*Biennial Survey of Education, 1928–1930*, United States Office of Education, Bulletin (1931) No. 20; Vol. I, Chapter II, p. 61.

[7]T. H. Briggs, "The Status of the Junior High School," *Educational Administration and Supervision*, 9:193–201, April, 1923.

T. H. Briggs, *The Junior High School*, pp. 50–54, Houghton Mifflin Company, 1920.

L. V. Koos, *op. cit.*, pp. 138–139, 494.

W. A. Smith, *The Junior High School*, pp. 325–327, The Macmillan Company, 1925.

[8]A somewhat different plan of organization was advocated by President Hutchins at the One Hundred Seventieth Convocation of the University of Chicago, December 20, 1932. See *School Review*, Vol. XLI, No. 2, February, 1933. President Hutchins states in part, "It is now clear that the work of that [the elementary] school can be completed in six years. After it, should come a secondary unit, definitely preparatory and not terminal in character, covering three or four years. Above the secondary school there should be a set of alternative courses of study, definitely terminal and not preparatory in character. They should cover not less than three and not more than four years. One of them should be devoted to general education. Others should deal with various types of technical training adapted to those who are not going on into professional schools of engineering or business but whose leanings are in these directions rather than toward general education.

"We should thus look forward to accommodating the educational needs of our population up to their eighteenth or twentieth year by six years of primary school, three or four years of secondary school, and three or four years of terminal courses of a technical or cultural kind. At the eighteenth or twentieth year the university should begin."

without incurring added expenses solely because of insufficient enrollment. That it might be done in smaller communities is not denied. A study of the junior high school in small communities was made in Massachusetts by Spaulding.[9] He indicates certain limitations and also certain possibilities for junior high schools of various types with various programs in schools with limited enrollments. Another study is needed in which the limitations and possibilities indicated by Spaulding are in some manner more specifically translated into actual costs.

The limitation was made to apply to cities with a total population of 5,000 or over, rather than to school systems with enrollments above a specified minimum because the total population classification is used by several state departments in their records and reports and it was therefore convenient to use it here. Although school enrollments do not tend to bear a fixed ratio to total population as between communities, no excessive variations were found in the very small schools in this study. Great variations were encountered, however, in several larger Massachusetts towns and cities where parochial schools absorbed almost half of the school enrollment.

### CURRENT EXPENSES

It was believed advisable further to limit the study to current expenses. Capital outlay is vital to a complete answer to the problem of junior high school costs but it involves issues of such magnitude and complexity as to merit separate investigation.

### PER PUPIL COSTS

The final limitation relates to per pupil costs as opposed to the total cost of education. Morrison[10] has indicated certain limitations in the use of unit costs, pointing out that "we shall have much use for the principle, but we must be on our guard as to what unit costs mean and what they do not mean. In general, they are a matter of relativistic rather than quantitative reasoning. The very common fallacy associated with their use is to treat a given unit cost as if it had real quantitative meaning." The primary

[9]F. T. Spaulding, *The Small Junior High School*, Harvard University Press, 1927.
[10]H. C. Morrison, *The Management of the School Money*, pp. 17, 392–393, University of Chicago Press, 1932.

use of per pupil costs in this investigation is that of relating costs in one unit of a school system or in one type of organization to costs in another unit or in another type of organization and as yet there is no method of reducing costs to a common basis better than that of costs per pupil.

Briggs, Childs,[11] and others by statement or implication have indicated that per pupil costs of junior high school education do not include all phases of the problem because the holding power of the reorganized school may tend to increase its total cost by increasing its total enrollment, or acceleration of pupils may tend to decrease its total costs, the effects of which might not be felt in per pupil costs. Childs[12] stated:

> Data . . . in another section of this investigation show that certain Indiana schools during the past five years have increased by as much as 18% the number of pupils who are retained through the seventh and eighth grades. In the large school this added retained list will add to the total cost for the system by necessitating more classes but not to the per capita cost, but in the small schools, whose class groups are below an economic standard size, the total cost will remain the same while the per capita cost will be actually decreased.

This whole matter of the effect of the junior high school organization upon total costs as distinguished from per pupil costs should be made the subject of further investigation. This study, however, is limited to per pupil costs and to conclusions which may be drawn therefrom.

Since per pupil costs may be based upon different types of units, such as pupils in average daily attendance, total enrollment, or number belonging, it was necessary to make a choice of the specific unit to be used. On the whole, present practice inclines toward the use of pupils in average daily attendance in reporting per pupil costs; therefore that method is used here.

In its limited form this study relates to per pupil costs[13] in aver-

---

[11]T. H. Briggs, *The Junior High School*, pp. 282–283.

H. G. Childs, *The Reorganization Movement in the Grammar Grades of Indiana Schools*, Fort Wayne Printing Company, 1918.

[12]*Ibid.*, p. 117.

[13]Although a distinction between costs and expenditures is sometimes made, as that made by Morrison, in which cost is defined as the "value in money of goods and services used up," and expenditure is defined as "payment out of revenue," the two terms are used synonymously throughout this investigation since it is "almost universally true that the net expenditures for the year as shown by the financial report are spoken of as the cost of the schools for the year and treated as such." Unless otherwise qualified both costs and expenditures mean "net expenditures" in this study. See H. C. Morrison, *op. cit.*, pp. 10–11.

age daily attendance for current expense in junior high schools organized on the 6–3–3 basis in cities of 5,000 or over.   Although in the beginning no limitations were set as to the geographical areas to be included in the study, it has been found advisable to limit it to six Eastern states: Connecticut, Massachusetts, New Jersey, New York, Pennsylvania, and Rhode Island.

# III

# Plan of the Investigation

IT HAS been found advisable to divide the investigation into four fairly distinct phases.

The first phase undertakes to establish the cost position of grades 7 to 9 in relation to grades K to 6 and grades 10 to 12 in the 6–3–3 systems in cities of more than 5,000 total population in six Eastern states. That is, it seeks to determine the common practices in supporting the junior high school unit as opposed to the practices in supporting the grades below and above it. Moreover, it examines in-so-far as is practicable in an extensive survey the reasons for such per pupil cost variations as are found existing between the junior high school unit and the grades below this unit; that is, between grades 7 to 9 and K to 6.

In the second phase an attempt is made to determine, in-so-far as it may be done by direct comparison, the effect of the 6–3–3 type of organization as distinguished from the 8–4 or traditional type of organization on school expenditures in all of the grades as a whole rather than on expenditures in those grades which are directly involved in the reorganization. In this phase the test of type of organization is the grouping of grades. In other words, the question is, how do average per pupil costs in grades K to 12 in 6–3–3 systems, irrespective of educational program, compare with average per pupil costs in grades K to 12 in 8–4 systems, regardless of educational program?

The purpose of the third phase is to measure the cost effect of the 6–3–3 type of organization on grades 7 to 9 as distinguished from the cost effect of the traditional or 8–4 type of organization upon these same grades, and to analyze to some extent the reasons for cost variations existing between the two types. The test of type of organization here as in the second phase is the grouping of grades, although in both phases it has been found that those systems which are 6–3–3 in organization tend to have many of the features of the ideal junior high school.[1]

[1]Certain features of the standard junior high school are given in Chapter IX.

The fourth phase is a critical examination of the cost implications of the various features of the standard junior high school. The first three phases are largely a question of the costs in 6–3–3 systems as these organizations actually exist and function, some offering few and some many of the features of ideal junior high school education, the test of organization being that of the grouping of grades. The fourth phase does not involve primarily junior high school education as it exists but junior high school education in its standard or more ideal form. There is, therefore, less attempt to support the fourth phase with an array of objective data such as are offered in the support of the first three.

The original plan of the investigation was to associate costs closely with the provision or lack of provision of the standard junior high school in each of the three phases. Soon after the actual field work was undertaken this plan was abandoned for two reasons. First, it was discovered that the mere provision for a feature did not guarantee that this feature functioned as was desired. For example, it was found that whereas special periods and special staff members were often designated for guidance or adjustment, sometimes little guidance work was done. Hence to associate costs with ideal junior high school education merely by relating costs to a check-list of features provided would in many instances prove futile, unless the functioning of these features might in some manner be measured. Second, the attention of the public in general and of those more immediately responsible for educational facilities, such as boards of education, superintendents, and principals, is largely focused upon the grouping of grades as the distinctive feature of junior high school education. That is, while there is realization that junior high school education is different in various ways from traditional, yet apparently the distinctive feature is the regrouping of grades. Moreover, costs are a major item in the issues of reorganization and therefore in the end the problem usually resolves itself into the question of how much it will cost to regroup the grades on the junior high school basis. This attitude is so prevalent that on every hand one finds many of the features of junior high school education provided by 8–4 systems which are unwilling to make the further change of complete reorganization. Largely for this second reason it was decided to place major emphasis upon the cost effects of the grouping of grades on the 6–3–3 basis, in the first three phases of the study, leaving for the fourth phase and for further studies the cost effects of the other distinguishing characteristics of standard junior high school education.

It has usually been assumed in past studies in this field that the first three phases indicated above are in fact one phase and that if it is established that grades 7 to 9 show higher per pupil costs than grades 1 to 6 in 6–3–3 systems, grades 7 to 9 in 6–3–3 systems will show higher per pupil costs than grades 7 to 9 in 8–4 systems, and that 6–3–3 systems probably will show higher per pupil costs as a whole than will 8–4 systems. No such assumptions are made here. It is believed that each of the above questions is a distinct phase of the problem and should be so treated.

The first phase although requiring much time and detailed work in the collection and checking of data is a relatively simple part of the study. Six states were selected which could be reached readily from New York City. Cost data were secured by character classification in grades K to 6, grades 7 to 9, and grades 10 to 12 separately for one hundred seven 6–3–3 systems located in the six selected states. These one hundred seven organizations consist of those 6–3–3 systems in which reorganization has been completed, that is, in which all pupils in grades 7 to 9 are enrolled in junior high schools; which are recognized as junior high schools by their respective state departments of education; and which are located in cities of greater than 5,000 total population. Data were secured for all the systems which met the above requirements in four of the states and for the great majority in the other two states. These data are reported by systems and by states in Chapter V.

To secure evidence bearing upon the second phase Massachusetts was selected for special investigation. Total and per pupil costs were secured by character classification in grades K to 12 for each 6–3–3 and for each 8–4 system in this state. Per pupil costs were also secured in grades K to 6, grades 7 to 9, and grades 10 to 12 in the 6–3–3 systems, and in grades K to 8 and grades 9 to 12 in the 8–4 systems. These data together with certain direct cost comparisons and interpretations are reported in Chapter VI.

It is in the third phase that the investigation meets a more complex situation. As has been indicated, it is here that an attempt is made to discover the cost effect of the 6–3–3 type of organization on grades 7 to 9 as distinguished from the cost effect of

the 8–4 type of organization on these same grades, without resorting to certain assumptions sometimes heretofore made and without
resorting to a direct cost comparison of the two types of organization.

### THE COST COMPARISON PLAN EMPLOYED

The difficulty to be met here is not unlike that so often encountered in educational research. The problem is to compare the
effects of two variables or of two groups of variables when these
variables operate in two uncontrolled situations, that is, when
variables other than those it is desired to compare or measure enter
into the situations. In this investigation it is desired to compare
the cost effects of having grades 7 to 9 organized on the traditional
plan with the cost effects of having them organized on the junior
high school plan. But to compare directly the costs in grades 7 to
9 in one type of organization with the costs in grades 7 to 9 in the
other type of organization probably ignores a variety of other
factors which contribute to the final determination of costs. One
common way out of the difficulty is to rule out all factors except
those two which are to be compared or measured, that is, to make
comparable the situations in which they operate. But what factors, other than the types of organization, may affect costs in
grades 7 to 9 in two different school situations? They are many
and highly important, such as those which have to do with wealth
or ability to support education, the desire and effort to support
education, the general level of the cost of living, and the like. It
might not be difficult to select a group of 6–3–3 systems for comparison with a group of 8–4 systems in which wealth and perhaps
even cost of living could be made reasonably comparable. However, when one considers such intangible and elusive factors as the
desire of the community to support education one is faced with
elements which it is difficult, if not impossible, to rule out. Moreover, this whole matter of the desire and effort of a community to
support education is associated to such an extent with so-called
progressive education and the latter is so much a part of the junior
high school movement that to attempt to rule out the factor of
effort to support education probably would tend to eliminate those
junior high schools which had adopted the most progressive pro-

grams of education. In other words, it seems that it might be impossible to rule out some factors which affect costs, other than types of organization, without affecting the selection of the two groups in such a way as to leave them unrepresentative of their respective groups.

Another approach to the problem is that of relating the variables to be compared or measured not directly with each other but with other variables which are of such a nature as to tend to eliminate or to equate for the irrelevant factors which it is desired to rule out of the situations. Such is the technique adopted here. And the other variables drawn into the situations by means of which it is hoped to eliminate the irrelevant factors are the per pupil costs of education in grades K to 6 in the 6–3–3 and 8–4 organizations which are compared. That is, the technique, which might be described as a ratio-of-costs comparison plan, consists in comparing the ratio of per pupil costs existing between grades K to 6 and grades 7 to 9 in certain selected 6–3–3 systems with the ratio of per pupil costs existing between grades K to 6 and grades 7 to 9 in certain selected 8–4 systems. The argument behind the plan is this: any cost differences existing between grades K to 6 and grades 7 to 9 in the same system will be due to differences between those units of grades and not to differences existing between communities. Thus there is secured two ratios which are independent of community differences.

The position taken here may be illustrated in this way: City A, a 6–3–3 organization, spends $75.00 per pupil in average daily attendance in grades K to 6 and $100.00 per pupil in grades 7 to 9; whereas City B, an 8–4 organization, spends $90.00 per pupil in grades K to 6 and $100.00 per pupil in grades 7 to 9. Why does City A spend only $75.00 per pupil in grades K to 6 while City B spends $90.00 per pupil? This difference is, of course, due to a variety of inter-community differences. Why does City A spend $100.00 in grades 7 to 9 and City B the same amount although there is a substantial variation in the per pupil expenditures in the grades below? This again is due to a variety of inter-community differences one of which may be the type of organization since City A is 6–3–3 and City B is 8–4. But this study does not attempt to separate those factors here designated as general inter-community differences from those which may be due to a difference in type of organization.[2]   Nor does this study rely on a method of direct cost comparison, such as drawing conclusions from a direct comparison of the per pupil costs in grades 7 to 9 in City A with the per pupil costs in these same grades in City B.   Rather, it seeks to answer the question, why does City A spend $25.00 more per pupil in grades 7 to 9 than in grades K to 6, whereas City B spends only $10.00 more per pupil in grades 7 to 9 than in grades K to 6?   The position is taken here, as indicated above, that the $25.00 difference in the case of City A and the $10.00 difference in the case of City B are due not to general inter-community differences since the grade units being compared are in the same system, but to different policies adopted in each community with respect to the financial support accorded grades 7 to 9 as opposed to that accorded grades K to 6.[3] It is also contended that if the amounts by which the per pupil costs in grades 7 to 9 exceed those in grades K to 6 are consistently higher in one type of organization than in another, such a situation may be taken as an indication that the per pupil costs in grades 7 to 9 are affected by type of organization.   However, no claim is made that valid conclusions may be drawn from the examination of a single pair of systems, nor is the claim made that fine distinctions may be drawn in dollars and cents from a comparison of two groups of systems.   But, to report the various policies of differentiating between the financial support accorded grades K to 6 and grades 7 to 9 specifically in terms of dollars and cents may be of value to those who contemplate a change from the 8–4 to the 6–3–3 type of organization.   That is, not only may a certain importance be attached to the fact that grades 7 to 9, in comparison with grades K to 6, may tend to be supported in one type of organization on a higher level than in the other, but likewise importance may be attached to the amounts involved.

It may be argued that there is a fallacy in the above plan of indirect cost comparison since grades K to 6 as a base for eliminating general inter-community cost differences may also tend to eliminate or to exaggerate differences due to type of organization.   That is,

[2]Difference in type of organization (6–3–3 as opposed to 8–4) may be considered as one of the various inter-community differences between two school systems.   However, since that is the variable which it is desired to measure or compare here, it is not classed as a general inter-community difference but as a specialized variation between systems, whereas all other differences are classed together as general inter-community differences.

[3]The reasons for different financial support being accorded these grade units are many and probably differ somewhat from community to community.   However, some of these reasons are given in later chapters and are not material here.

if shifting from the 8–4 to the 6–3–3 plan should operate to raise or lower per pupil costs in grades K to 6 then these latter grades would not be a good base on which to compare the cost tendencies of grades 7 to 9. This problem was anticipated and given attention throughout the third phase of the investigation. In no case was it found that the per pupil costs in the grades below the junior high school were affected materially by shifting from the 8–4 to the 6–3–3 plan. This statement is not based on the fact that per pupil costs in grades K to 6 in the new 6–3–3 system were the same as per pupil costs in grades K to 8 before the change. In almost every situation examined the per pupil costs in grades K to 6 after the change were lower than per pupil costs had been in grades K to 8. This seemed to indicate an influence of type of organization on per pupil costs in grades K to 6. However, a careful examination of this issue in several instances revealed that costs in grades K to 6 were lower than they had been in grades K to 8, apparently not because grades K to 6 were affected by the change,[4] but because the removal of grades 7 and 8 from the K to 8 unit left the K to 6 unit with lower costs. This was one of the first indications that perhaps all the facts were not known relative to the costs of grades K to 6 as distinguished from the costs of grades 7 and 8 in 8–4 schools.

In the above description of the indirect method of cost comparison reference is constantly made to grades 7 to 9 as though they constituted a distinct unit of grades in 8–4 systems as they do in 6–3–3 systems. This, of course, is not the case, grades 7 and 8 being integral parts of the unit made up of grades K to 8, and grade 9 constituting a part of grades 9 to 12. However, it was necessary to select corresponding groups for purposes of comparison. Since the junior high school unit is composed of grades 7 to 9 one method would be to maintain this unit intact and to throw grades 7, 8, and 9 together in the 8–4 systems. Another method would be to maintain grades 7 and 8 as a separate unit distinct from grade 9 in the 8–4 systems since they were segregated from different groups, and then to break up the costs of grades 7 to 9 in the junior high schools into one unit of grades 7 and 8, and another unit of grade 9 and thus secure corresponding groups. The initial plan was to employ both methods. However, it was later decided to abandon the second plan and to compare grades

---

[4] A careful examination indicated that personnel, salaries, class size, program of studies, and the like were practically unmodified in grades K to 6 by the change from the 8–4 to the 6–3–3 organization.

7 to 9 as a single junior high school unit with grades 7 to 9 as a combined unit in 8–4 systems. This decision was made for several reasons. First, great difficulty was encountered in segregating the costs in grade 9 from the costs in grades 7 and 8 in the junior high schools. Second, in those 6–3–3 systems where the costs of grade 9 were segregated from grades 7 and 8 it was discovered that there was very little variation. Third, the relative importance of grades 7 and 8 as distinguished from grade 9 in determining costs in grades 7 to 9 in 8–4 systems can be shown without making a comparison with these same grades in 6–3–3 systems, which even if done would mean little since costs in grade 9 in 6–3–3 systems tend to be approximately the same as in grades 7 and 8.

Since the plan of the fourth phase is to discuss the cost implications of various features of the standard junior high school, it has been found necessary to set up a tentative standard organization. This is done largely by drawing from the literature in the field. In some cases certain evidence or illustrative materials are drawn from the data secured for the first three phases. On the whole, however, the plan of the fourth phase is a general though critical discussion of the cost implications of those essential features of the reorganized school which in the opinion of authorities contribute to ideal junior high school education.

# IV

# Securing the Cost Data

THE data for the first phase of the investigation, which reports per pupil costs in grades K to 6, 7 to 9, and 10 to 12 in one hundred seven 6–3–3 systems and examines certain causes for cost variations between grades K to 6 and grades 7 to 9 in these systems, were secured from the original financial reports filed by the local schools with the state departments of education, and from some field work which brought direct contact with the local organizations. Connecticut, Massachusetts, and Rhode Island have recently adopted systems of state financial reports which require that all reorganized schools make their financial reports on the basis of the new organization rather than on the 8–4 basis. For many years the 6–3–3 systems of these states reported their expenditures as though they were 8–4 organizations. The state departments were reluctant to make provision for junior high school financial reports as long as there were few clear-cut reorganized systems. New York and Pennsylvania make provision for their reorganized schools to report on the junior high school basis their major items of expenditure, such as for salaries of teachers, principals, and supervisors, for textbooks and instructional supplies, for operation and for maintenance. New Jersey makes no provision for a direct report, by the local systems to the state department, of such a nature as to be of great use in this investigation. However, the local school systems of New Jersey make comprehensive reports of receipts and expenditures to the county superintendents. Those systems whose organizations vary from the 8–4 type no longer report expenditures as 8–4 schools; they report for the elementary school, the junior high school, and the senior high school as separate units.

For Connecticut, Massachusetts, and Rhode Island all the data reported here were secured by a careful examination of original financial reports filed in the state departments of education. The major part of the data reported here for New York and Pennsylvania was secured in the same manner.   However, it was necessary to secure added information by means of correspondence with or visits to local systems in order to allocate certain items of expenditure to the elementary grades and to the junior and senior high school units.   In the case of New Jersey some data were secured from the state department of education and from certain county superintendents, but many were secured by means of field work in the state.

It was possible to include in this first phase of the investigation every accredited, completely reorganized 6–3–3 system located in communities of more than 5,000 population in Connecticut, Massachusetts, New York, and Rhode Island.   Because of the difficulties involved in securing the data, it was necessary to omit several systems in Pennsylvania and approximately one-fourth in New Jersey.[1]

In addition to a careful scrutiny of the financial reports themselves, the instructions issued by the various state departments for making cost allocations were examined and on that basis cost reallocations were made to conform to the usual character classification.[2]   On the whole it was not necessary to re-allocate many items.

Just how accurate the local systems were in making the division of costs between grades K to 6, 7 to 9, and 10 to 12 and in the allocation of costs to the various categories in the character classification is not, of course, known.   However, such checks were at hand as to assure a reasonable degree of accuracy at least in the major items of expense.   Moreover, the reports of many of the state departments are so organized and so checked as not to encourage the mere prorating of expenditures.

For the second phase, in which per pupil costs in grades K to 12 in the 6–3–3 systems of a single state are compared directly with per pupil costs in grades K to 12 in the 8–4 systems of the same state, financial information was obtained by securing in Massachusetts,

---

[1]It is not mandatory in Pennsylvania that junior high school systems report separately for the elementary grades, the junior high school, and the senior high school.   A few 6–3–3 schools still make grades K to 8 and grades 9 to 12 the basis of their reports.   It was not feasible to include these schools.

It was particularly difficult to secure cost data in New Jersey because the information desired for this investigation is on file in the state department of education by counties rather than by local districts.   It was not feasible to include every system in the field work of the state and correspondence was often unsatisfactory.   However, the great majority of the 6–3–3 organizations of the state were finally included.

[2]F. Engelhardt and F. Von Borgersrode, *Accounting Procedure for School Systems*, p. 32, Bureau of Publications, Teachers College, Columbia University, 1927.

in addition to the data already gathered from the 6–3–3 systems, similar information from the 8–4 schools of that state. Since the financial data in the 8–4 systems are reported for two separate units, grades K to 8 and 9 to 12, whereas such data in the 6–3–3 systems are reported for three separate units, grades K to 6, 7 to 9, and 10 to 12, and since thus the units do not include the same grades, the cost data are not comparable between types of organization for any unit of grades less than K to 12. However, this phase of the investigation deals primarily with the expenditures of the school systems as a whole for each type of organization rather than with the expenditures of certain grades.

It was in the third phase of the investigation that real difficulty was encountered in securing the desired cost data. Twenty-four school systems—twelve 6–3–3 and twelve 8–4—were selected for special study. The purpose of this special study, as has already been indicated, was to make an indirect comparison of per pupil costs in grades 7 to 9 in 6–3–3 organizations with per pupil costs in grades 7 to 9 in traditional or 8–4 organizations. This necessitated that per pupil costs for grades 7 to 9 be made available in 8–4 systems as well as in 6–3–3 systems. Herein lay the major difficulty, because whereas costs were reported for grades 7 to 9 as a separate unit in 6–3–3 systems, costs for grades 7 to 9 either as individual grades or as a separate unit of the three grades combined were not available in 8–4 systems since the costs in grades 7 and 8 were reported as a part of the unit composed of grades K to 8 and costs in grade 9 were reported as a part of the unit composed of grades 9 to 12. The only recourse was to make a field investigation of the twelve 8–4 systems and with all available data thus at hand to segregate the costs in grades 7 and 8 from those in grades K to 8 and the costs in grade 9 from those in grades 9 to 12.

Since the costs were to be analyzed ultimately on the basis of character classification and since the cost accounts of practically all school systems are organized on the character basis, the segregation of the costs in grades 7 and 8 and in grade 9 was made on that basis. Costs for instruction other than salaries, although usually not carried as a separate division in the classification of expenditures according to character, are included as a separate category here. Hence, costs for grades 7 to 9 were segregated from the elementary grades and the high school in 8–4 systems on the basis of general control; instructional costs, salaries; instructional costs other than salaries; operation; maintenance; coördinate activities; auxiliary agencies; fixed charges.

## INSTRUCTIONAL COSTS, SALARIES

The salaries of teachers, supervisors, and principals were charged to grades 7 and 8 and to grade 9 in the 8–4 systems on the basis of the time spent in those grades. When the elementary school was departmentalized it was not difficult to compute the salaries chargeable to grades 7 and 8 because the majority of the teachers assigned to those grades spent no portion of their time elsewhere. However, there were usually part-time teachers, special teachers, special subject supervisors, regular supervisors, and substitutes whose salaries had to be allocated on the basis of the time spent in the various grades. In most instances accurate information was available in the office of the superintendent of schools regarding the activities (including division of time between grade units) of these special teachers and supervisors. In some instances it was found satisfactory to charge salaries of special teachers in some manner other than by computing the proportion of time spent in the various grades. For example, in the case of supervisors who dealt only with teachers, it was often necessary to apportion salaries according to the number of teachers in the grades with which the supervisors were concerned.

Elementary schools only partly departmentalized, and especially platoon schools, presented great difficulties. In these cases the majority of teachers having classes in grades 7 and 8 usually had classes in other grades also. For this reason it was necessary to take each teacher as a special case and carefully determine the time spent in grades 7 and 8 and then to charge salaries accordingly.

The salaries of principals were charged on the basis of the number of teachers in grades 7 and 8, on the theory that the principal deals more with teachers as units than with pupils. However, the number of teachers usually bears some relationship to the number of pupils in a grade, therefore the results would not be greatly different if the time of the principal had been prorated according to the number of pupils rather than teachers.

Grade 9 always presented a task of considerable magnitude. Whereas certain high school teachers often spend much of their time in grade 9, few are assigned exclusively to that grade. Hence, as in the case of some elementary schools, it was necessary to trace the time of the majority of the teachers who had ninth grade classes. It was not enough to know how much time was spent in grade 9; it was necessary to know how much time was spent elsewhere also. If a teacher spent two periods in grade 9 and three periods in grade 10, two-fifths of her time was charged to grade 9; but if she spent two periods in grade 9 and four periods in grade 10 then only one-third of her time could be charged to grade 9.

The task became very involved and almost impossible of achievement when the salaries of special teachers, such as those of physical education and music, were allocated. The difficulty here was not only that these teachers usually covered so much territory but that often their classes were mixtures of several grades. Classes in harmony and chorus as a rule include pupils from several grades· And gymnasium classes are formed usually on the basis of sex rather than of grades. Moreover, some of the regular academic classes presented the same difficulties. It was not uncommon to find freshmen and sophomores in the same Latin and social science classes, and it was the rule rather than the exception in the smaller schools to find mixed grades in much of the commercial work. In such instances salaries were charged to grade 9 in proportion to the number of ninth grade pupils. The task, which required considerable patience, could always be brought to a satisfactory close although in many instances the salary of a single teacher, because of her varied schedule and her mixed classes, was allocated by being multiplied by numerous fractions.

It might be objected at this point that such great care in allocating instructional salaries to grades 7 and 8 and to grade 9 in 8–4 schools could not be warranted by any possible use to which the results might be put. However, accuracy is always better than inaccuracy no matter what use is made of the results. Moreover, by far the largest item of cost in schools is that of expenditures for instructional salaries. Slight errors here and there plus the "guessing attitude" could easily result in sums of considerable size. And it should be recalled that these figures are used for comparative purposes and therefore each error would have double significance. If $5,000 too much is charged to grades 7 and 8, whereas it should be charged to grades K to 6, this means that a sum $5,000 too large will be compared with a sum $5,000 too small. The extreme rapidity with which small errors and omissions piled up into large sums convinced the investigator that only the greatest effort toward accuracy would bring anything like worth-while results in this study.

## GENERAL CONTROL

This charge must always be prorated in some manner if it is to be allocated to separate grades, or grade divisions.   Common practice in state reports seems to be shifting from prorating on the basis of the number of pupils to prorating on the basis of the number of teachers.[3]   The latter practice is followed here because of its convenience and because it is believed that the offices of the board of education and the superintendent of schools find their time claimed by problems which deal more directly with teachers than with pupils as units.

Allocating general control costs to grades 7 and 8 and to grade 9 was easily accomplished since the number of teachers chargeable to these grades had been computed carefully in allocating salaries. Principals, supervisors, and special teachers of all kinds were included with regular teachers in determining the final figures for each unit of grades.

## INSTRUCTIONAL COSTS, OTHER THAN SALARIES

This group of expenditures includes textbooks and supplies and all items of expense directly connected with the offices of principals, supervisors, or heads of departments, such as clerical help, traveling expenses, and the like.   Only rarely were the expenditures in grades 7 and 8 for textbooks and supplies carried as cost accounts separate from those of the lower grades.   However, it was possible to estimate the expenditures for grades 7 and 8 with considerable accuracy because the majority of school systems have adopted policies whereby they set aside certain amounts in their budgets each year for textbooks and supplies for lower grades, intermediate grades, and upper grades.   Where this was not done it was necessary to make the estimate by going over the yearly expenditures and segregating the items chargeable to grades 7 and 8.   Usually

---

[3] The financial reports required of the local school systems by some of the state departments of education call for general control to be reported as a single item for the whole system and not to be allocated to the various grade units.

this could be done without great difficulty because the textbooks furnished in the upper grades were readily distinguishable from those used in the lower grades and on the whole the supplies could be traced by means of the requisition blanks. This latter method of estimating was always used for grade 9. Expenditures connected with the offices of principals, supervisors, and heads of departments, including either regular or part-time clerical help, were prorated on the basis of the number of teachers chargeable to grades 7 and 8 and to grade 9.

## OPERATION OF PLANT

The costs of operating the plant were computed on the basis of total space used by grades 7 and 8 and by grade 9, and not prorated on the basis of average daily attendance as is often done. To prorate on such a basis would be futile for the purposes of this investigation since it would show the same per pupil costs for each pupil in the same building regardless of class size or of variations in size of rooms occupied by different classes.

The matter was relatively simple when grades 7 and 8 occupied the same rooms throughout the day, or when they did little shifting from room to room. But in the case of departmentalization (the teachers usually being assigned definite rooms and the pupils changing) which extended below grade 7, and especially in the case of the platoon system, it was necessary to compute on the basis of actual time spent in various rooms. In the majority of schools the sizes of the rooms were taken directly from the blue-prints of the buildings. Occasionally it was necessary to measure some class-rooms.

In the ninth grade it was found that the total number of classes per week was an excellent index of space occupied.[4] That is, the total space used by grades 9 to 12 was computed and the per cent of that space chargeable to grade 9 was the per cent that ninth grade classes were of all high school classes. This was tested in several schools and found to be quite accurate, the only error being due to the fact that a little too much space might be charged to the ninth grade since the upper grades used the larger rooms, such as

[4] The week was used rather than the day because all classes did not meet daily and in order to compute accurately the per cent that all ninth grade classes were of all high school classes it was necessary to take a time unit that included the meeting of all classes.

commercial rooms, laboratories, and special rooms, proportionately
more than the ninth grade. However, no large errors were found
in the cases tested.

### MAINTENANCE OF PLANT

The costs of maintenance were charged in the same manner as
were the costs of operation—in proportion to the space occupied by
the grades in question. In most instances this proved to be a
satisfactory method because the major items of maintenance usually affect a building as a whole rather than the portion of a building occupied exclusively by certain grades. Where grades 7 and 8
occupied separate buildings an attempt was made to get the actual
maintenance costs for those buildings.

### COÖRDINATE ACTIVITIES

When school nurses kept records indicating the number and the
grades of the pupils given dental and medical care during the year
it was possible to estimate accurately the proportion of cost chargeable to grades 7 and 8, and to grade 9. Likewise, where medical
and dental service consisted only of inspection in definite grades it
was not difficult to allocate costs. However, in some cases it was
necessary to charge costs on the basis of the opinions of teachers,
principals, nurses, physicians, and dentists as to time spent and as
to the proportion of supplies furnished. Since, on the whole, it was
found that opinions in each of such schools were fairly uniform it
is believed that any division of costs based thereon is not greatly in
error.

### AUXILIARY AGENCIES

It was found that in the schools of this investigation one of the
principal items chargeable to auxiliary agencies was that of transportation. This could be accurately allocated because usually
very definite records were kept of pupils transported, or of money
advanced for transportation. Items such as lunch room deficits
and expenditures in connection with public libraries were prorated
on the basis of pupils. Other items as playground and athletic
costs could often be definitely charged to specific grades. Where
grades 7 and 8 were housed in separate buildings, as they sometimes

were for the entire city, it was possible to segregate costs for all auxiliary agencies with great accuracy.

### FIXED CHARGES

In the 8–4 schools investigated it was found that insurance and pensions constituted practically the only items in fixed charges. Since insurance was almost always fire insurance on school buildings the most equitable basis of division of costs seemed to be the total space occupied by the grades in question. The costs of teachers' pensions to the local systems could be allocated readily to the desired grades since a record is kept of the pension payments made to the fund of each individual teacher.

Securing the cost data for the twelve 6–3–3 systems was a much less difficult task than for the twelve 8–4 systems since in every case grades 7 to 9 constituted a separately organized unit for which separate cost accounts were kept. The exact manner of allocating costs, however, was examined and in some cases re-allocations were made in order to conform to the method used in the 8–4 systems. Changes were made particularly in the division of salaries of supervisors and special teachers whose duties took them into the several grade units of the system. Too often it was discovered that it was common practice to charge the entire salary of a supervisor to that school unit where she was first assigned and where apparently she spent the major portion of her time although in fact she spent much of her time in either or both of the other divisions.

It should be understood that the care exercised in obtaining the cost data for the twenty-four cities of opposing types of organization was directed primarily toward the correct division of costs between grades K to 6, 7 to 9, and 10 to 12 rather than toward the correct allocation of costs according to character classification. The latter was the method of analyzing costs in order to attain the former. Nevertheless, whereas the chief purpose behind the method used was the attainment of a correct division of expenditures between the grade units, this method was selected because it provides a convenient means of analyzing costs for another purpose, that of showing in what significant ways, if any, the per pupil costs in grades 7 to 9 vary as between the two types of organization.

Although the same means of allocating costs were employed in the 6–3–3 schools as in the 8–4 organizations there is one important way in which the data differed when finally secured for the twenty-four systems. It is obvious that because of the necessity for segregating the costs of grades 7 and 8 from grades K to 8 and the costs of grade 9 from grades 9 to 12 in the 8–4 schools, the costs for those schools would be available for grades 7 and 8 separate from grade 9. It is equally obvious that because the costs were secured for the 6–3–3 schools in units of grades K to 6, 7 to 9, and 10 to 12 costs for grades 7 and 8 would not be available separate from the costs for grade 9. Therefore the cost data for grades 7 to 9 in the 8–4 schools, being in two separate units, were not in a form comparable to the cost data for grades 7 to 9 in the 6–3–3 systems. It was, however, a relatively simple matter to combine the costs in grades 7 and 8 with the costs in grade 9 in the 8–4 systems and thus to secure a unit comparable with that in the 6–3–3 systems. In Chapter VII the per pupil costs in the twelve 8–4 organizations are reported for grades 7 and 8 and for grade 9 separately as well as in combined form.

The fourth phase, which is a discussion of the cost implications of the various features of the standard junior high school, is supported at points by certain objective data which were secured during the field work for the other three phases. However, no systematic attempt was made to secure data to illustrate or to support positions taken relative to the various cost issues which are raised in the fourth phase.

# V

# Cost of the Junior High School as a Unit in the 6–3–3 Type of Organization

THIS phase of the investigation is made a part of the study for three reasons: first, for the purpose of determining for a considerable geographical area, by systems, by states, and by population groups, the common financial practice of supporting the junior high school unit in the 6–3–3 type of organization; second, to make a brief analysis of the major reasons why per pupil costs show variations between grades K to 6 and grades 7 to 9 in 6–3–3 systems; third, in order to offer some information relative to the common assumption that since grades 7 to 9 show a higher per pupil expenditure than grades K to 6 in 6–3–3 systems, the junior high school organization is more costly than the traditional 8–4 type.

For this part of the investigation data were drawn from one hundred seven 6–3–3 systems located in six eastern states. As has already been indicated these organizations constitute all the accredited 6–3–3 systems in communities of more than 5,000 population in four of these states and the great majority in the two other states. Forty-two are located in Massachusetts, twenty in Pennsylvania, eighteen in New Jersey, sixteen in New York, six in Rhode Island, and five in Connecticut. The surprisingly small number of 6–3–3 organizations in all the states except Massachusetts is due partly to the population limit set in this study, but primarily to the fact that only "pure" 6–3–3 systems are included, and many schools of each state have not accomplished complete reorganization. Some of the well-known junior high school systems of the East, such as Rochester, New York, were not included for this reason. The junior high school system operates side by side with the 8–4 organization in New York City, Philadelphia, and Boston; in such communities as Providence,[1] Worcester, New

[1]Providence has completed reorganization to the 6–3–3 plan since the data were secured for this study.

Haven, Bridgeport, Schenectady, Albany, Syracuse, Jersey City; and in many other cities of considerable population. An interesting study would be to report costs for the two types of organization as they operate in these dual systems. However, in many instances these schools are transitional in nature and it is doubtful if their costs would be representative of the well-stabilized junior high school system.

Table 1 presents for the school year 1930–1931[2] the costs per pupil in average daily attendance for current expenses in grades K to 6,[3] 7 to 9, and 10 to 12 for one hundred seven 6–3–3 systems. The range of per pupil costs is considerable for each unit of grades,

TABLE 1

COSTS PER PUPIL IN AVERAGE DAILY ATTENDANCE IN GRADES K TO 6, 7 TO 9, 10 TO 12, AND K TO 12 FOR ONE HUNDRED SEVEN 6–3–3 SYSTEMS IN SIX EASTERN STATES

| SYSTEM* | STATE | COST PER PUPIL | | | |
| --- | --- | --- | --- | --- | --- |
| | | Grades K–6 | Grades 7–9 | Grades 10–12 | Grades K–12 |
| 1. | Rhode Island | $ 47.67 | $ 99.12 | $164.04 | $ 73.95 |
| 2. | Pennsylvania | 54.25 | 72.42 | 106.07 | 71.21 |
| 3. | Rhode Island | 57.69 | 88.84 | 141.14 | 69.96 |
| 4. | Rhode Island | 57.89 | 148.74 | 125.06 | 82.47 |
| 5. | Pennsylvania | 59.30 | 95.70 | 116.41 | 80.67 |
| 6. | Pennsylvania | 63.02 | 79.05 | 97.46 | 75.39 |
| 7. | Massachusetts | 64.91 | 105.08 | 136.49 | 85.06 |
| 8. | Pennsylvania | 66.82 | 124.23 | 144.37 | 85.86 |
| 9. | Pennsylvania | 67.74 | 76.88 | 108.04 | 77.46 |
| 10. | New York | 67.97 | 87.72 | 105.78 | 85.20 |
| 11. | Pennsylvania | 68.19 | 96.41 | 159.40 | 87.76 |
| 12. | Pennsylvania | 69.02 | 141.82 | 138.34 | 94.41 |
| 13. | Pennsylvania | 70.37 | 116.37 | 131.05 | 91.20 |
| 14. | Pennsylvania | 70.69 | 128.34 | 133.20 | 91.97 |
| 15. | Massachusetts | 70.91 | 98.40 | 134.32 | 89.01 |
| 16. | Pennsylvania | 71.08 | 120.82 | 170.43 | 95.75 |
| 17. | Massachusetts | 71.13 | 85.23 | 164.78 | 91.93 |
| 18. | Massachusetts | 71.46 | 118.38 | 139.53 | 94.61 |
| 19. | Massachusetts | 71.56 | 104.07 | 103.35 | 84.78 |
| 20. | Massachusetts | 71.92 | 127.24 | 185.51 | 96.90 |
| 21. | Pennsylvania | 72.22 | 110.47 | 142.73 | 93.18 |
| 22. | Pennsylvania | 72.50 | 100.14 | 159.30 | 90.75 |
| 23. | Rhode Island | 72.63 | 113.04 | 176.75 | 94.55 |
| 24. | Rhode Island | 73.85 | 84.95 | 142.13 | 89.36 |

*See footnote, p. 38.

[2]In several instances the per pupil costs reported for Pennsylvania systems are for the school year 1929–1930. [3]In those cases where no kindergarten work is offered the per pupil costs for the lower unit are for grades 1 to 6.

TABLE 1 (*Continued*)

| SYSTEM* | STATE | COST PER PUPIL | | | |
|---|---|---|---|---|---|
| | | Grades K–6 | Grades 7–9 | Grades 10–12 | Grades K–12 |
| 25. | Massachusetts | $ 73.89 | $ 80.37 | $105.00 | $ 79.93 |
| 26. | Massachusetts | 74.27 | 79.43 | 120.84 | 82.56 |
| 27. | Massachusetts | 74.59 | 118.07 | 135.61 | 95.12 |
| 28. | Massachusetts | 74.85 | 98.38 | 136.88 | 89.24 |
| 29. | Massachusetts | 75.11 | 123.42 | 135.29 | 91.94 |
| 30. | Connecticut | 76.32 | 119.19 | 117.37 | 92.11 |
| 31. | Massachusetts | 76.35 | 103.84 | 141.61 | 93.01 |
| 32. | Massachusetts | 76.45 | 74.13 | 161.87 | 90.60 |
| 33. | Massachusetts | 76.84 | 88.82 | 126.97 | 90.38 |
| 34. | Massachusetts | 77.05 | 106.26 | 120.56 | 91.27 |
| 35. | Massachusetts | 78.02 | 102.69 | 147.49 | 94.41 |
| 36. | Massachusetts | 78.21 | 91.65 | 156.97 | 89.78 |
| 37. | Massachusetts | 78.22 | 90.68 | 185.72 | 96.91 |
| 38. | Massachusetts | 78.29 | 104.39 | 151.03 | 93.72 |
| 39. | Rhode Island | 78.60 | 89.01 | 131.14 | 86.92 |
| 40. | Massachusetts | 78.83 | 96.32 | 127.14 | 92.82 |
| 41. | Connecticut | 79.31 | 115.88 | 151.37 | 96.49 |
| 42. | Massachusetts | 79.90 | 99.24 | 129.34 | 92.69 |
| 43. | Massachusetts | 81.04 | 92.71 | 122.65 | 91.07 |
| 44. | Pennsylvania | 81.37 | 80.18 | 115.39 | 85.93 |
| 45. | Pennsylvania | 83.57 | 92.73 | 151.45 | 95.50 |
| 46. | Pennsylvania | 84.27 | 144.75 | 142.22 | 111.17 |
| 47. | Massachusetts | 84.79 | 78.30 | 184.64 | 99.03 |
| 48. | Massachusetts | 85.13 | 95.97 | 113.03 | 91.44 |
| 49. | Massachusetts | 86.40 | 120.89 | 130.03 | 95.77 |
| 50. | Massachusetts | 86.45 | 117.65 | 121.77 | 100.99 |
| 51. | New York | 88.34 | 120.95 | 158.97 | 106.51 |
| 52. | Massachusetts | 88.59 | 111.51 | 179.97 | 108.06 |
| 53. | Massachusetts | 89.15 | 112.42 | 129.74 | 100.73 |
| 54. | Massachusetts | 89.16 | 155.66 | 141.25 | 115.74 |
| 55. | Massachusetts | 89.33 | 117.17 | 163.65 | 103.64 |
| 56. | Pennsylvania | 89.49 | 147.37 | 211.04 | 115.17 |
| 57. | Massachusetts | 89.51 | 112.77 | 171.99 | 111.15 |
| 58. | New Jersey | 89.64 | 138.42 | 135.46 | 112.91 |
| 59. | Massachusetts | 89.78 | 126.63 | 176.98 | 112.40 |
| 60. | Massachusetts | 89.85 | 114.07 | 132.90 | 97.98 |
| 61. | Pennsylvania | 89.87 | 100.03 | 94.85 | 93.09 |
| 62. | Massachusetts | 90.40 | 93.07 | 169.57 | 104.87 |
| 63. | New Jersey | 91.52 | 144.31 | 178.61 | 114.65 |
| 64. | Massachusetts | 91.65 | 112.87 | 144.41 | 103.98 |
| 65. | Massachusetts | 93.23 | 148.57 | 207.94 | 124.09 |
| 66. | Pennsylvania | 93.39 | 122.06 | 200.51 | 118.83 |
| 67. | Massachusetts | 95.90 | 135.06 | 168.17 | 117.98 |
| 68. | Massachusetts | 95.97 | 137.57 | 170.59 | 121.85 |
| 69. | Connecticut | 96.23 | 129.96 | 120.77 | 108.61 |
| 70. | New York | 98.29 | 116.77 | 144.69 | 109.87 |

## TABLE 1 (*Continued*)

| SYSTEM* | STATE | Grades K–6 | Grades 7–9 | Grades 10–12 | Grades K–12 |
|---|---|---|---|---|---|
| | | COST PER PUPIL | | | |
| 71. | New York | $ 98.72 | $123.34 | $134.25 | $113.02 |
| 72. | New York | 99.56 | 131.34 | 124.40 | 110.97 |
| 73. | New York | 100.01 | 107.09 | 112.87 | 104.62 |
| 74. | New York | 100.07 | 89.25 | 149.94 | 108.10 |
| 75. | Massachusetts | 100.45 | 96.96 | 191.66 | 116.04 |
| 76. | Connecticut | 101.59 | 158.68 | 157.47 | 124.01 |
| 77. | Massachusetts | 102.19 | 124.06 | 161.68 | 117.47 |
| 78. | Massachusetts | 102.89 | 140.20 | 194.31 | 127.09 |
| 79. | New Jersey | 103.71 | 138.01 | 163.17 | 113.89 |
| 80. | New Jersey | 104.72 | 131.41 | 161.58 | 121.11 |
| 81. | New York | 107.84 | 145.44 | 133.03 | 119.07 |
| 82. | New Jersey | 111.58 | 165.66 | 156.38 | 134.41 |
| 83. | Pennsylvania | 113.95 | 136.91 | 218.22 | 142.59 |
| 84. | New Jersey | 114.17 | 176.51 | 227.24 | 148.95 |
| 85. | New Jersey | 114.25 | 157.11 | 178.07 | 132.65 |
| 86. | New Jersey | 114.29 | 176.52 | 180.34 | 142.88 |
| 87. | New Jersey | 115.48 | 133.28 | 200.14 | 132.78 |
| 88. | New Jersey | 117.33 | 119.54 | 236.28 | 129.18 |
| 89. | New Jersey | 118.03 | 158.37 | 196.51 | 139.25 |
| 90. | Connecticut | 120.22 | 149.83 | 178.84 | 134.69 |
| 91. | New York | 120.61 | 123.02 | 126.85 | 122.32 |
| 92. | New York | 121.83 | 164.99 | 135.94 | 136.09 |
| 93. | New York | 122.20 | 140.35 | 191.37 | 141.43 |
| 94. | New Jersey | 122.98 | 143.02 | 173.87 | 141.11 |
| 95. | Massachusetts | 124.15 | 171.83 | 225.17 | 152.07 |
| 96. | New York | 130.87 | 144.72 | 207.24 | 144.78 |
| 97. | New Jersey | 135.70 | 218.90 | 206.18 | 181.04 |
| 98. | New Jersey | 144.15 | 197.83 | 218.03 | 176.99 |
| 99. | New Jersey | 147.19 | 205.89 | 243.26 | 179.35 |
| 100. | New York | 152.29 | 232.92 | 264.91 | 192.11 |
| 101. | New Jersey | 160.25 | 244.21 | 268.66 | 198.00 |
| 102. | New York | 160.44 | 194.39 | 225.44 | 178.93 |
| 103. | Pennsylvania | 164.98 | 208.16 | 234.42 | 184.50 |
| 104. | New Jersey | 174.90 | 165.16 | 166.77 | 171.01 |
| 105. | New York | 185.76 | 265.71 | 250.20 | 213.51 |
| 106. | New Jersey | 187.30 | 220.07 | 260.66 | 209.47 |
| 107. | New York | 287.91 | 355.50 | 411.70 | 325.63 |
| | MEAN | 96.23 | 128.80 | 162.23 | 114.46 |
| | MEDIAN | 89.16 | 119.54 | 151.45 | 103.98 |

*The systems are given numbers in the order of ascending costs in the elementary grades from system 1 with a cost of $47.67 to system 107 with a cost of $287.91. The name of the system is not given because wide variations in cost might lead to unfair interpretations or criticisms of expenditures since all of the facts are not given here as to why costs vary between systems. For example, in many metropolitan areas living costs alone account for high school costs. Yet this might not be given due consideration in interpreting cost variations between systems. However, complete cost data are on file for these 107 systems by name.

from $47.67 to $287.91 in grades K to 6, from $72.42 to $355.50 in grades 7 to 9, and from $94.85 to $411.70 in grades 10 to 12. The mean per pupil costs in grades 7 to 9 are $128.80, almost to the dollar midway between the mean per pupil costs in grades K to 6 of $96.23, and the mean per pupil costs in grades 10 to 12 of $162.23. Although in each unit of grades the median is somewhat lower than the mean, the cost position of grades 7 to 9 in relation to grades K to 6 and 10 to 12 is practically the same when the median is used as a measure of central tendency as when the mean is used.

Because the mean and the median indicate a tendency for systems with the 6–3–3 type of organization to accord financial support to grades 7 to 9 at a figure approximately midway between the figures for grades K to 6 and 10 to 12 this should not be interpreted as indicating that junior high school costs fall approximately midway between the costs in grades K to 8 and grades 9 to 12 in 8–4 organizations. That is, the cost relationship here indicated should not be taken as a basis by means of which 8–4 systems might predict possible costs in grades 7 to 9 in 6–3–3 organizations. The fact that costs in grades 7 to 9 tend to take this position midway between costs in grades K to 6 and 10 to 12 in 6–3–3 systems is not evidence that costs in grades 7 to 9 in newly organized 6–3–3 systems will tend to fall midway between costs in grades K to 8 and 9 to 12 prior to reorganization.

The coefficient of correlation, computed by the product-moment method, between the per pupil costs in grades K to 6 and in 7 to 9 for the one hundred seven 6–3–3 systems is .89; the correlation between per pupil costs in grades K to 6 and in 10 to 12 is .80; and the correlation between per pupil costs in grades 7 to 9 and in 10 to 12 is .80. This indicates that for these 6–3–3 organizations there is considerable tendency for those systems with high costs in one unit of grades to have high costs in all units of grades and a similar tendency for those systems with low costs in one unit of grades to have low costs in all units of grades. Perhaps this is to be expected. However, there has long been a feeling in connection with the junior high school movement that the junior high schools on the whole present wide differences and vary greatly from community to community, and that elementary and regular secondary, and perhaps senior high school education, being more stabilized and standardized probably would tend to exhibit fewer variations than junior high school education. It appears, however, that in so far as costs can be taken as an indication of type of educational program, the correlation shown here is some evidence that junior high school education does not vary from community to community with little or no relationship to elementary education as has been supposed, since there is this tendency for junior high school education to be supported on a high level when elementary education is so supported and on a low level when elementary education is so supported.[4]  It is interesting to note that the correlation between grades K to 6 and 7 to 9 is higher than between grades K to 6 and 10 to 12.   This might be interpreted as showing that those factors which determine the support accorded elementary education tend to enter into the determination of the support accorded junior high school education more than they enter into the senior high school situation.

Other interpretations might be made from the high correlation shown between costs in grades K to 6 and 7 to 9, such as that junior high school education may not be greatly different from elementary.   However, Table 1 shows that the junior high school level of costs is substantially above that of the elementary unit. Perhaps a more reasonable interpretation would be that community wealth, community desire to support education, geographic locale, and such other factors as determine the educational program of the elementary school also are important factors in determining the junior high school educational program.

It is difficult to interpret relative costs from the actual cost data shown in Table 1; Table 2 has therefore been produced.   In this table per pupil costs in grades K to 6 in each of the 107 systems are given an index value of 100 and per pupil costs in the other grade units are given proportional values.

Table 2 shows that the mean per pupil costs in grades 7 to 9 for the one hundred seven 6–3–3 systems are 133.8 when mean per pupil costs in grades K to 6 are 100; that is, junior high school per pupil costs are on the average 33.8 per cent higher than elementary. Per pupil costs in grades 10 to 12 are 68.6 per cent higher than in K

[4]Since this correlation is between two similar factors there might be the temptation to conclude similarity between absolute costs in the two types of organization.   When height is correlated with weight, or size of head with I.Q., for example, it is easily apparent that the coefficient of correlation shows nothing as to the absolute weight or height, or as to the actual intelligence quotient or size of head. Likewise, the high coefficient of correlation between per pupil costs for two units of grades shows nothing as to the actual levels of costs in the two units, but indicates a tendency for low costs in one unit to be accompanied by low costs in the other unit, and vice versa, but low costs in the junior high school unit may be on a much higher level than low costs in grades K to 6.

TABLE 2

RELATIVE COSTS PER PUPIL IN AVERAGE DAILY ATTENDANCE IN GRADES K
TO 6, 7 TO 9, 10 TO 12, AND K TO 12, FOR ONE HUNDRED SEVEN 6–3–3
SYSTEMS IN SIX EASTERN STATES

| SYSTEM | STATE | RATIO OF PER PUPIL COSTS WHEN COSTS IN GRADES K–6 EQUAL 100 | | | |
|--------|-------|------------|------------|--------------|--------------|
| | | Grades K–6 | Grades 7–9 | Grades 10–12 | Grades K–12 |
| 74. | New York | 100 | 89.2 | 149.8 | 108.0 |
| 47. | Massachusetts | 100 | 92.3 | 217.8 | 116.8 |
| 104. | New Jersey | 100 | 94.4 | 95.4 | 97.8 |
| 75. | Massachusetts | 100 | 96.5 | 190.8 | 115.5 |
| 32. | Massachusetts | 100 | 97.0 | 211.7 | 118.5 |
| 44. | Pennsylvania | 100 | 98.5 | 141.8 | 105.6 |
| 88. | New Jersey | 100 | 101.9 | 201.4 | 110.1 |
| 91. | New York | 100 | 102.0 | 105.2 | 101.4 |
| 62. | Massachusetts | 100 | 102.9 | 187.6 | 116.0 |
| 26. | Massachusetts | 100 | 106.9 | 162.7 | 111.2 |
| 73. | New York | 100 | 107.1 | 112.9 | 104.6 |
| 25. | Massachusetts | 100 | 108.8 | 142.1 | 108.2 |
| 96. | New York | 100 | 110.6 | 158.4 | 110.6 |
| 45. | Pennsylvania | 100 | 111.0 | 181.2 | 114.3 |
| 61. | Pennsylvania | 100 | 111.3 | 105.5 | 103.6 |
| 48. | Massachusetts | 100 | 112.7 | 132.8 | 107.4 |
| 39. | Rhode Island | 100 | 113.2 | 166.8 | 110.6 |
| 9. | Pennsylvania | 100 | 113.5 | 159.5 | 114.3 |
| 43. | Massachusetts | 100 | 114.4 | 151.4 | 112.4 |
| 93. | New York | 100 | 114.8 | 156.6 | 115.7 |
| 24. | Rhode Island | 100 | 115.0 | 192.5 | 121.0 |
| 87. | New Jersey | 100 | 115.4 | 173.3 | 115.0 |
| 33. | Massachusetts | 100 | 115.6 | 165.2 | 117.6 |
| 37. | Massachusetts | 100 | 115.9 | 237.4 | 123.9 |
| 94. | New Jersey | 100 | 116.3 | 141.4 | 114.7 |
| 36. | Massachusetts | 100 | 117.2 | 200.7 | 114.8 |
| 106. | New Jersey | 100 | 117.5 | 139.2 | 111.8 |
| 70. | New York | 100 | 118.8 | 147.2 | 111.8 |
| 17. | Massachusetts | 100 | 119.8 | 231.7 | 129.2 |
| 83. | Pennsylvania | 100 | 120.1 | 191.5 | 125.1 |
| 102. | New York | 100 | 120.2 | 140.5 | 111.5 |
| 77. | Massachusetts | 100 | 121.4 | 158.2 | 114.9 |
| 40. | Massachusetts | 100 | 122.2 | 161.3 | 117.7 |
| 64. | Massachusetts | 100 | 123.1 | 157.6 | 113.4 |
| 107. | New York | 100 | 123.5 | 143.0 | 113.1 |
| 42. | Massachusetts | 100 | 124.2 | 161.9 | 116.0 |
| 90. | Connecticut | 100 | 124.6 | 148.8 | 112.0 |
| 71. | Pennsylvania | 100 | 124.9 | 136.0 | 114.5 |
| 6. | Pennsylvania | 100 | 125.4 | 154.6 | 119.6 |
| 80. | New Jersey | 100 | 125.5 | 154.3 | 115.6 |
| 52. | Massachusetts | 100 | 125.9 | 202.9 | 122.0 |
| 57. | Massachusetts | 100 | 126.0 | 192.1 | 124.2 |

TABLE 2 (*Continued*)

| SYSTEM | STATE | Grades K–6 | Grades 7–9 | Grades 10–12 | Grades K–12 |
|---|---|---|---|---|---|
| | | RATIO OF PER PUPIL COSTS WHEN COSTS IN GRADES K–6 EQUAL 100 | | | |
| 53. | Massachusetts | 100 | 126.1 | 145.5 | 113.0 |
| 103. | Pennsylvania | 100 | 126.2 | 142.1 | 111.8 |
| 60. | Massachusetts | 100 | 127.0 | 147.9 | 109.0 |
| 10. | New York | 100 | 129.1 | 155.6 | 125.3 |
| 66. | Pennsylvania | 100 | 130.7 | 214.7 | 127.2 |
| 55. | Massachusetts | 100 | 131.2 | 183.2 | 116.0 |
| 28. | Massachusetts | 100 | 131.4 | 182.9 | 119.2 |
| 35. | Massachusetts | 100 | 131.6 | 189.0 | 121.0 |
| 72. | New York | 100 | 131.9 | 124.9 | 111.5 |
| 79. | New Jersey | 100 | 133.1 | 157.3 | 109.8 |
| 38. | Massachusetts | 100 | 133.3 | 192.9 | 119.7 |
| 2. | Pennsylvania | 100 | 133.5 | 195.5 | 131.3 |
| 89. | New Jersey | 100 | 134.2 | 166.5 | 118.0 |
| 81. | New York | 100 | 134.9 | 123.4 | 110.4 |
| 69. | Connecticut | 100 | 135.0 | 125.5 | 112.9 |
| 92. | New York | 100 | 135.4 | 111.6 | 111.7 |
| 31. | Massachusetts | 100 | 136.0 | 185.5 | 121.8 |
| 50. | Massachusetts | 100 | 136.1 | 140.9 | 116.7 |
| 78. | Massachusetts | 100 | 136.3 | 188.8 | 123.5 |
| 51. | New York | 100 | 136.9 | 179.9 | 120.6 |
| 98. | New Jersey | 100 | 137.2 | 151.2 | 122.8 |
| 85. | New Jersey | 100 | 137.5 | 155.9 | 116.1 |
| 34. | Massachusetts | 100 | 137.9 | 156.5 | 118.4 |
| 22. | Pennsylvania | 100 | 138.1 | 219.7 | 125.2 |
| 95. | Massachusetts | 100 | 138.4 | 181.4 | 122.5 |
| 15. | Massachusetts | 100 | 138.8 | 189.4 | 125.5 |
| 99. | New Jersey | 100 | 139.9 | 165.3 | 121.8 |
| 49. | Massachusetts | 100 | 140.0 | 150.5 | 110.8 |
| 67. | Massachusetts | 100 | 140.8 | 175.4 | 123.0 |
| 59. | Massachusetts | 100 | 141.0 | 197.1 | 125.2 |
| 11. | Pennsylvania | 100 | 141.4 | 233.8 | 128.7 |
| 105. | New York | 100 | 143.0 | 134.7 | 114.9 |
| 68. | Massachusetts | 100 | 143.3 | 177.7 | 127.0 |
| 19. | Massachusetts | 100 | 145.4 | 144.4 | 118.5 |
| 41. | Connecticut | 100 | 146.1 | 190.9 | 121.7 |
| 82. | New Jersey | 100 | 148.5 | 140.1 | 120.5 |
| 101. | New Jersey | 100 | 152.4 | 167.6 | 123.6 |
| 100. | New York | 100 | 152.9 | 173.9 | 126.1 |
| 21. | Pennsylvania | 100 | 153.0 | 197.6 | 129.0 |
| 3. | Rhode Island | 100 | 154.0 | 244.6 | 121.2 |
| 86. | New Jersey | 100 | 154.4 | 157.8 | 125.0 |
| 58. | New Jersey | 100 | 154.4 | 151.1 | 126.0 |
| 84. | New Jersey | 100 | 154.6 | 199.0 | 130.5 |
| 23. | Rhode Island | 100 | 155.6 | 243.4 | 130.2 |
| 30. | Connecticut | 100 | 156.2 | 153.8 | 120.7 |

TABLE 2 (*Continued*)

| SYSTEM | STATE | RATIO OF PER PUPIL COSTS WHEN COSTS IN GRADES K–6 EQUAL 100 | | | |
|---|---|---|---|---|---|
| | | Grades K–6 | Grades 7–9 | Grades 10–12 | Grades K–12 |
| 76. | Connecticut | 100 | 156.2 | 155.0 | 122.1 |
| 63. | New Jersey | 100 | 157.7 | 195.2 | 125.3 |
| 27. | Massachusetts | 100 | 158.3 | 181.8 | 127.5 |
| 65. | Massachusetts | 100 | 159.4 | 223.0 | 133.1 |
| 97. | New Jersey | 100 | 161.3 | 151.9 | 133.4 |
| 5. | Pennsylvania | 100 | 161.4 | 196.3 | 136.0 |
| 7. | Massachusetts | 100 | 161.9 | 210.3 | 131.0 |
| 29. | Massachusetts | 100 | 164.3 | 180.1 | 122.4 |
| 56. | Pennsylvania | 100 | 164.7 | 235.8 | 128.7 |
| 13. | Pennsylvania | 100 | 165.4 | 186.2 | 129.6 |
| 18. | Massachusetts | 100 | 165.7 | 195.3 | 132.4 |
| 16. | Pennsylvania | 100 | 170.0 | 239.8 | 134.7 |
| 46. | Pennsylvania | 100 | 171.8 | 168.8 | 131.9 |
| 54. | Massachusetts | 100 | 174.6 | 158.4 | 129.8 |
| 20. | Massachusetts | 100 | 176.9 | 257.9 | 134.7 |
| 14. | Pennsylvania | 100 | 181.5 | 188.4 | 130.1 |
| 8. | Pennsylvania | 100 | 185.9 | 216.1 | 128.5 |
| 12. | Pennsylvania | 100 | 205.4 | 200.4 | 136.8 |
| 1. | Rhode Island | 100 | 207.9 | 344.1 | 155.1 |
| 4. | Rhode Island | 100 | 256.9 | 216.0 | 142.5 |
| | MEAN | 100 | 133.8 | 168.6 | 118.9 |
| | MEDIAN | 100 | 133.5 | 167.6 | 119.7 |

to 6; hence the percentage by which per pupil costs in the senior high school exceed those in the elementary is approximately double the percentage by which per pupil costs in the junior high school exceed those in the elementary. In each unit of grades the median closely approximates the mean.

However, the range of cost differences between grade units is considerable. In System 74 the per pupil costs in grades 7 to 9 are actually less than in grades K to 6, being only 89.2 per cent as great; whereas in System 4 grades 7 to 9 exhibit per pupil costs which are 156.9 per cent higher than costs in grades K to 6. It will be noted that six systems show a lower cost in grades 7 to 9 than in grades K to 6, and six systems show a cost in grades 7 to 9 which is more than 75 per cent higher than in grades K to 6. The costs in Table 2 are relative costs and should not be confused with actual or absolute costs. For example, System 107, with a junior high school cost which is higher than that shown by any other system in grades 7 to 9 (see Table 1), shows a relative cost for this grade unit which is only 23.5 per cent higher than that of the elementary grades. System 1, with a junior high school cost of only $99.12, which is considerably below the mean for the 107 systems, shows a relative cost in these grades that is 107.9 per cent above the costs in grades K to 6, which is, except for System 4, the highest percentage shown for any junior high school.

Since one of the purposes of this phase of the investigation is to determine the reasons for per pupil cost variations between grades 7 to 9 and grades K to 6, it is pertinent to ask why System 4 spends 156.9 per cent more per pupil in the junior high school than in the elementary school, when System 74 or System 47 spends less in grades 7 to 9 than in grades K to 6. And it would be interesting to know why System 12, which spends only $69.02 per pupil in the lower grades, spends $141.82 in the junior high school, while System 104, which spends $174.90 in the lower grades, spends only $165.16 in grades 7 to 9. However, these are only individual cases which show the extremes; and while it would be valuable to indicate what determines costs in grades 7 to 9 as opposed to costs in grades K to 6 for each of these 107 systems, there is not sufficient space available to do this. They can better be thrown into convenient classes or groups for interpretative analysis. One method of grouping is by states which has the added advantage of showing cost variations between the six states.

Table 3 presents by states, for the school year 1930–1931, the costs per pupil in average daily attendance for current expenses in

TABLE 3

COSTS PER PUPIL IN AVERAGE DAILY ATTENDANCE IN GRADES K TO 6, 7 TO 9, 10 TO 12, AND K TO 12, FOR ONE HUNDRED SEVEN 6–3–3 SYSTEMS IN SIX EASTERN STATES, BY STATES

| STATE | NUMBER OF SYSTEMS | COST PER PUPIL | | | |
|---|---|---|---|---|---|
| | | Grades K–6 | Grades 7–9 | Grades 10–12 | Grades K–12 |
| Connecticut | 5 | $ 86.49 | $126.69 | $140.43 | $103.41 |
| Massachusetts | 42 | 84.55 | 110.01 | 147.42 | 100.05 |
| New Jersey | 18 | 114.86 | 161.59 | 192.07 | 136.63 |
| New York | 16 | 127.14 | 162.88 | 169.44 | 142.77 |
| Pennsylvania | 20 | 81.37 | 118.23 | 159.48 | 101.44 |
| Rhode Island | 6 | 66.93 | 108.09 | 152.76 | 86.38 |
| Six States | 107 | 94.37 | 128.76 | 160.31 | 112.26 |

grades K to 6, 7 to 9, and 10 to 12 for the one hundred seven 6–3–3 organizations. This table shows the results obtained by considering pupils rather than school systems as units. That is, the expenditures of all the 6–3–3 systems for each state were added and this sum divided by the total average daily attendance. Likewise, the results reported in this table for the six states combined were obtained in the same manner; the total expenditures of all the states were added and this sum was divided by the total average daily attendance of all the states. Such a procedure gives more weight to the states with more or larger 6–3–3 systems, such as Massachusetts, than to the states with fewer or smaller systems, such as Connecticut. It should be noted in Table 3 that the results reported for the various grade units for the six states combined are not identical with the means shown for the one hundred seven 6–3–3 systems in Table 1. This is because the means of the latter table are derived by adding the per pupil costs, not the total costs, in the 107 systems and dividing this sum by 107, which gives equal weight to each system regardless of size. In Table 3 the systems lose their identity and total expenditures are divided by total average daily attendance for each unit of grades. While the results are not identical in the two tables they do not vary greatly. The difference in grades 7 to 9 is very small, $128.80 per pupil in average daily attendance when the systems are given equal weight, and $128.76 per pupil in average daily attendance when the systems are weighted. This indicates that great differences would not be found to exist between the per pupil expenditures in grades 7 to 9 in the smaller systems as a whole and the per pupil expenditures in grades 7 to 9 in the larger systems as a whole.

In Table 4 the results shown in Table 3 are reproduced in the form of relative costs. Per pupil costs in grades K to 6 for each state are given an index value of 100 and the per pupil costs in other grade units are given proportional values. Interpreted in per cents it means that in Connecticut per pupil costs in grades 7 to 9 are 46.5 per cent higher than in grades K to 6. Similar interpretations may be made for the other grade units and for the other states.

The cost variations between the grade units show large differences from state to state. In New York per pupil costs in grades 7 to 9 are only 28.1 per cent above those in grades K to 6, whereas in Rhode Island the variation is 61.5 per cent, considerably more than double the variation in New York. Even greater differences appear in the senior high school; costs in these grades exceed those in the elementary school by only 33.3 per cent in New York, but by 128.2 per cent in Rhode Island. These per cents indicate that

TABLE 4

RELATIVE COSTS PER PUPIL IN AVERAGE DAILY ATTENDANCE IN GRADES K TO 6, 7 TO 9, 10 TO 12, AND K TO 12, FOR ONE HUNDRED SEVEN 6-3-3 SYSTEMS IN SIX EASTERN STATES, BY STATES

| STATE | RATIO OF PER PUPIL COSTS WHEN COSTS IN GRADES K TO 6 EQUAL 100 | | | |
|---|---|---|---|---|
| | Grades K-6 | Grades 7-9 | Grades 10-12 | Grades K-12 |
| Connecticut | 100 | 146.5 | 162.4 | 119.5 |
| Massachusetts | 100 | 130.1 | 174.4 | 118.4 |
| New Jersey | 100 | 140.7 | 167.2 | 118.9 |
| New York | 100 | 128.1 | 133.3 | 112.3 |
| Pennsylvania | 100 | 145.3 | 196.0 | 124.7 |
| Rhode Island | 100 | 161.5 | 228.2 | 129.1 |
| Six States | 100 | 136.4 | 169.9 | 119.0 |

there is no common practice in the six selected states as to the policy followed in supporting grades 7 to 9 in relation to the support accorded grades K to 6 or grades 10 to 12.

New York spends $162.88 per pupil in grades 7 to 9, the highest of the six states; Rhode Island spends $108.09, the lowest of the six states. Yet in relation to expenditures in grades K to 6 New York spends the least in grades 7 to 9 and Rhode Island spends the most, as is indicated by Table 4. It is true, of course, that the whole picture involves the low costs in grades K to 6 in Rhode Island in comparison with the high costs in grades K to 6 in New York. That, however, is not the issue here. The question is, why does Rhode Island spend 61.5 per cent more per pupil in grades 7 to 9 than in grades K to 6 when New York spends only 28.1 per cent more? It is a question of the policy of supporting one unit of grades as opposed to the policy of supporting another unit of grades. If Rhode Island can support a system of elementary education by expending $66.93 per pupil, then why must she spend $108.09 per pupil in the junior high school? Likewise, if it requires an expenditure of $127.14 per pupil in New York to maintain a satisfactory system of elementary education, how can New York adequately support her junior high schools on an expenditure of

$162.88 per pupil? Differences in cost of living and in wealth
of communities cannot account for these variations. Between
New York and Rhode Island there appears to be a rather fundamental difference in the policy of supporting the junior high school
as opposed to the policy of supporting the elementary school.
Although the sharpest differences are seen in these two states the
variations in policy between some of the others, as in the neighboring states of Connecticut and Massachusetts, are not insignificant.

When state divisions are disregarded and the one hundred seven
6–3–3 systems are thrown into population groups, as shown in
Table 5, the extreme variations in actual as well as in relative per
pupil costs are smoothed out. The per pupil costs in grades K to 6

TABLE 5

COSTS PER PUPIL IN AVERAGE DAILY ATTENDANCE IN GRADES K TO 6, 7 TO 9,
10 TO 12, AND K TO 12 FOR ONE HUNDRED SEVEN 6–3–3 SYSTEMS,
BY POPULATION GROUPS

| POPULATION GROUP | NUMBER OF SYSTEMS | COST PER PUPIL | | | |
|---|---|---|---|---|---|
| | | Grades K–6 | Grades 7–9 | Grades 10–12 | Grades K–12 |
| More than 100,000 | 10 | $93.60 | $126.08 | $163.41 | $109.81 |
| 30,000–100,000 | 35 | 94.71 | 133.29 | 157.91 | 113.26 |
| 10,000–30,000 | 42 | 94.74 | 122.06 | 164.41 | 112.85 |
| 5,000–10,000 | 20 | 94.02 | 126.44 | 151.80 | 113.65 |
| ALL GROUPS | 107 | 94.37 | 128.76 | 160.31 | 112.26 |

are almost identical in the different groups; costs in grades 10
to 12 do not differ greatly; and it is only in the case of the 30,000 to
100,000 population group that grades 7 to 9 show considerable
variation.

One may see readily from Table 6 that there are no significant
trends between population groups in supporting grades 7 to 9
as opposed to grades K to 6. The variation in costs between
these two grade units is identical to a per cent in the largest and
smallest population groups, and the highest and lowest variations
are found in the two central population groups.

Although this classification on a population basis indicates
clearly that there are no significant cost trends within the grade
units from one population group to another, and although it shows
but little difference from one group to another in the variation of
costs between grades 7 to 9 and grades K to 6, such a classification

## 48 Junior High School Costs

does not, of course, wipe out the variations which actually exist
between cities and between states in the policy of supporting the
junior high school as opposed to the elementary school in 6–3–3
organizations.

The financial data for the one hundred seven 6–3–3 systems show
that per pupil costs in the junior high schools exceed consistently,
though in varying amounts, the per pupil costs in the elementary
schools in the same systems. One of the major purposes of this

TABLE 6

RELATIVE COSTS PER PUPIL IN AVERAGE DAILY ATTENDANCE IN GRADES K
TO 6, 7 TO 9, 10 TO 12, AND K TO 12 FOR ONE HUNDRED SEVEN 6 3 3
SYSTEMS IN SIX EASTERN STATES, BY POPULATION GROUPS

| POPULATION GROUP | RATIO OF PER PUPIL COSTS WHEN COSTS IN GRADES K TO 6 EQUAL 100 | | | |
| --- | --- | --- | --- | --- |
| | Grades K–6 | Grades 7–9 | Grades 10–12 | Grades K–12 |
| More than 100,000 | 100 | 134.7 | 174.6 | 117.3 |
| 30,000–100,000 | 100 | 140.7 | 166.7 | 119.6 |
| 10,000–30,000 | 100 | 128.8 | 173.5 | 119.1 |
| 5,000–10,000 | 100 | 134.5 | 161.4 | 120.9 |
| ALL GROUPS | 100 | 136.4 | 169.9 | 119.0 |

phase of the investigation is to determine the elements or factors
which contribute to this situation. Classification by states (as in
Tables 8 and 9) provides a convenient number of groups by means
of which to examine these factors of cost variations. In grouping
the various systems by states, rather than giving each system equal
weight, the total expenditures for the systems in each state are
divided by the total average daily attendance in each state. Likewise, where the data reported are for the one hundred seven systems combined (as in Table 7) the computations are made on the
basis of total expenditures divided by total average daily attendance rather than on the basis of equal weight to each system.

One method of examining the factors which contribute to cost
variations between grade units is to analyze expenditures by
character classification. This is done in Table 7 for the 107 systems combined. This table shows in terms of the character
classification of expenditures why per pupil costs in grades 7 to 9
are $128.76 when the per pupil costs in grades K to 6 are only
$94.37. It shows that in every item except that of coördinate

activities the costs in grades 7 to 9 exceed the costs in grades K to 6. Moreover, it indicates that the cost differences between these grade units are not large in *actual amounts* for any items except instruction and operation, and that, as would be expected, instructional costs alone account for the major part of the cost variations. However, while many of the character items show

TABLE 7

COSTS PER PUPIL IN AVERAGE DAILY ATTENDANCE IN GRADES K TO 6, 7 TO 9, 10 TO 12, AND K TO 12 FOR ONE HUNDRED SEVEN 6–3–3 SYSTEMS COMBINED, BY CHARACTER

| ITEM | COST PER PUPIL | | | |
| --- | --- | --- | --- | --- |
| | Grades K–6 | Grades 7–9 | Grades 10–12 | Grades K–12 |
| General Control | $ 3.44 | $ 4.26 | $ 4.61 | $ 3.80 |
| Instruction | 70.17 | 99.31 | 125.85 | 85.30 |
| Operation | 10.92 | 13.66 | 17.23 | 12.51 |
| Maintenance | 4.08 | 4.49 | 5.33 | 4.37 |
| Coördinate Activities | 2.12 | 1.70 | 1.45 | 1.92 |
| Auxiliary Agencies | 1.60 | 2.59 | 2.77 | 2.00 |
| Fixed Charges | 2.04 | 2.75 | 3.07 | 2.36 |
| TOTAL | $94.37 | $128.76 | $160.31 | $112.26 |

small actual differences between these two units of grades, from the standpoint of relative costs many of them are substantial. The actual difference for auxiliary agencies is only $0.99 and yet per pupil costs in grades 7 to 9 exceed per pupil costs in grades K to 6 by 62 per cent for this item.

A different and perhaps a clearer picture of the situation is shown by Table 8 which gives not the actual costs for each unit of grades by character but the differences in actual costs between grades K to 6 and grades 7 to 9 by character for the six states. It shows, for example, that in Connecticut general control costs are $0.36 higher per pupil in grades 7 to 9 than in grades K to 6. It shows, likewise, that for this same item in Pennsylvania the variation in costs between grades K to 6 and 7 to 9 is $1.38. It also indicates that in every state per pupil expenditures are higher in grades 7 to 9 than in grades K to 6 for general control, instruction, operation, and auxiliary agencies, but that in two states costs are lower in the junior high school than in the elementary school for maintenance and for fixed charges and in all the states costs are lower for coördinate activities. Moreover, it shows that in at least three states operation is a factor of considerable importance in explaining higher junior high school costs but that by far the most important item in every state is that of instruction.

### TABLE 8

AMOUNTS THAT COSTS IN GRADES 7 TO 9 EXCEED COSTS IN GRADES K TO 6 IN ONE HUNDRED SEVEN 6–3–3 SYSTEMS IN SIX EASTERN STATES, BY CHARACTER

| ITEM | STATES | | | | | | |
|---|---|---|---|---|---|---|---|
| | Conn. | Mass. | N. J. | N. Y. | Pa. | R. I. | Six States |
| General Control | $ .36 | $ .52 | $ .94 | $ .93 | $ 1.38 | $ .76 | $ .82 |
| Instruction | 35.46 | 23.10 | 39.69 | 29.51 | 28.66 | 34.64 | 29.14 |
| Operation | 1.65 | 1.27 | 3.76 | 2.70 | 4.72 | 4.57 | 2.74 |
| Maintenance | 2.46 | — .35* | .83 | 1.06 | .73 | — .09 | .41 |
| Coördinate | —1.01 | — .58 | — .39 | — .07 | — .28 | — .47 | — .42 |
| Auxiliary | 1.24 | .87 | 2.01 | .16 | .59 | 2.08 | .99 |
| Fixed Charges | .04 | .62 | — .11 | 1.46 | 1.06 | — .33 | .71 |
| TOTAL | $40.20 | $25.45 | $46.73 | $35.75 | $36.86 | $41.16 | $34.39 |

*Minus indicates higher costs in grades K to 6 than in grades 7 to 9 and therefore should be subtracted.

Just how important the various character items are in explaining cost differences is indicated, but not clearly shown, by Table 8. Table 9 gives, not the actual amounts, but the per cents which the various character items contribute to the per pupil cost differences between grades 7 to 9 and K to 6. That is, counting the $40.20

### TABLE 9

PER CENT THAT EACH ITEM, BY CHARACTER, CONTRIBUTES TO TOTAL EXCESS OF COSTS IN GRADES 7 TO 9 OVER K TO 6, IN ONE HUNDRED SEVEN 6–3–3 SYSTEMS IN SIX EASTERN STATES

| ITEM | STATE | | | | | | |
|---|---|---|---|---|---|---|---|
| | Conn. | Mass. | N. J. | N. Y. | Pa. | R. I. | Six States |
| General Control | .9 | 2.1 | 2.0 | 2.6 | 3.7 | 1.8 | 2.4 |
| Instruction | 88.2 | 90.8 | 84.9 | 82.6 | 77.7 | 84.2 | 84.7 |
| Operation | 4.1 | 5.0 | 8.0 | 7.5 | 12.8 | 11.1 | 8.0 |
| Maintenance | 6.1 | — 1.4* | 1.8 | 3.0 | 2.0 | — .2 | 1.2 |
| Coördinate | — 2.5 | — 2.3 | .8 | .2 | — .7 | — 1.1 | — 1.2 |
| Auxiliary | 3.1 | 3.4 | 4.3 | .4 | 1.6 | 5.0 | 2.9 |
| Fixed Charges | .1 | 2.4 | — .2 | 4.1 | 2.9 | — .8 | 2.0 |
| TOTAL | 100.0 | 100.0 | 100.0 | 100.0 | 100.0 | 100.0 | 100.0 |

*Minus indicates higher cost in grades K to 6 than in grades 7 to 9 and therefore should be subtracted.

which measures in Connecticut the total excess of costs in grades 7 to 9 over costs in grades K to 6 (see Table 8) as 100 per cent, general control contributes .9 per cent, instruction 88.2 per cent, operation 4.1 per cent, maintenance 6.1 per cent, auxiliary agencies 3.1 per cent, and fixed charges .1 per cent to this total, while coördinate activities call for a subtraction of 2.5 per cent from the total, because this item shows a smaller cost in grades 7 to 9 than in grades K to 6. The magnitude of the item of instruction will be seen at once.  It ranges from 77.7 per cent in Pennsylvania to 90.8 per cent in Massachusetts with an average of 84.7 per cent for the six states.

Since instruction accounts for approximately 85 per cent of the difference in costs between the junior high school unit and the elementary unit in the one hundred seven 6–3–3 systems, a closer examination of this item should reveal further causes for cost differences.  For this purpose instructional costs are divided into two groups; first, costs due to the salaries paid all regular and special teachers, supervisors, and principals; and second, costs due to expenditures for textbooks, library books, instructional supplies, expenses of principals, supervisors, and teachers, and for salaries of all regular or special clerical help granted principals, supervisors, or teachers.  The purpose of this division of instructional costs is to segregate for closer examination the salaries paid those directly connected with classroom instruction.

Although the various items of expenditure indicated above include all groups of instructional costs, such items will not account wholly for differences in per pupil instructional costs between two units of grades.  The ratio of pupils to teachers also enters into the situation.  That is, higher average salaries per teacher in grades 7 to 9 than in grades K to 6 would tend to make per pupil costs higher in the former unit of grades than in the latter, but fewer pupils per teacher in the junior high school unit than in the elementary unit would have the same effect.  Hence for a closer scrutiny of per pupil cost differences for instruction, three elements are examined here: first, all instructional salaries (excluding clerical salaries); second, all other expenses of instruction (including clerical salaries); and third, pupil-staff ratio.[5]

It was not feasible to segregate expenditures chargeable to in-

[5]Since all teachers, supervisors, and principals are included for the purpose of computing average salaries and of computing the ratio of pupils to teachers, perhaps a better expression of the situation is pupil-staff ratio rather than pupil-teacher ratio.  When the former term is used it refers to the ratio o pupils to the entire staff of the school.  The latter term is used in its usual sense.

structional salaries from other instructional expenditures for all the 6–3–3 systems of New Jersey. For this reason it was believed advisable to omit New Jersey from this part of the analysis rather than to report for a smaller number of systems than were originally included in this state. Hence, cost data for five states instead of for six will be reported in the remaining tables of this chapter.

In Table 10 there is shown by states the per cents that instructional salaries and instructional costs other than salaries contribute to the total difference in costs between grades 7 to 9 and grades K to 6 in five eastern states. That is, if the $40.20, by which the cost of the junior high school unit exceeds that of the elementary unit in Connecticut, equals 100 per cent, 6.7 per cent of this amount is due to instructional costs other than teachers' salaries, and 81.5 per cent is due to instructional salaries. For the five states 10.0 per cent of the higher costs of grades 7 to 9 is due to

TABLE 10

PER CENT THAT INSTRUCTIONAL SALARIES, INSTRUCTIONAL COSTS OTHER THAN SALARIES, AND TOTAL INSTRUCTIONAL COSTS CONTRIBUTE TO TOTAL AMOUNT COSTS IN GRADES 7 TO 9 EXCEED COSTS IN GRADES K TO 6 IN FIVE EASTERN STATES

| ITEM | STATE | | | | | |
|---|---|---|---|---|---|---|
| | Conn. | Mass. | N. Y. | Pa. | R. I. | Five States |
| Instruction—Salaries only | 81.5 | 78.9 | 75.4 | 66.1 | 75.9 | 74.7 |
| Instruction—Other costs | 6.7 | 11.9 | 7.2 | 11.6 | 8.3 | 10.0 |
| Instruction—Total | 88.2 | 90.8 | 82.6 | 77.7 | 84.2 | 84.7 |

instructional costs other than salaries and 74.7 per cent is due to instructional salaries.

It might seem that it is implied by the foregoing statement that if the same average salaries were paid to the junior high school staff as to the elementary staff in these five states, approximately 75 per cent of the cost difference between grades 7 to 9 and K to 6 would be eliminated. However, as has been indicated, the actual salaries paid are only one factor in accounting for cost difference between these two grade units. The other factor is the number of pupils per staff member, or the pupil-staff ratio. That is, since the costs considered in this investigation are costs per pupil in average daily attendance, the mere adjustment between grades 7 to 9 and K to 6 of salaries paid per staff member would not equalize per pupil costs for instructional salaries between these grade units unless there were the same number of pupils per staff member. Hence to account for 75 per cent of the cost difference between grades K to 6 and grades 7 to 9 in the five eastern states requires that pupil-staff ratio as well as average salary per staff member be considered.

Table 11 gives the pupil-staff ratio for grades K to 6 and 7 to 9 for the five states and Table 12 gives the average salaries paid staff members in grades K to 6 and 7 to 9 for the same states. These tables indicate that in New York, for example, there are 4.5 fewer pupils per staff member in the junior high schools than in the elementary schools and that staff members in the junior high schools receive, on the average, $149.79 more than staff members in the elementary schools. These facts are significant in opening up the problem of junior high school costs. That is, if in the junior high schools of New York there were 4.5 more pupils per staff member and each member of the staff received $149.79 less than at present, the salary costs per pupil for instruction would be identical in grades K to 6 and 7 to 9 and *at least* 75.4 per cent of the per pupil cost difference between these two units of grades would be removed for that state.

The statement that at least 75.4 per cent of the total cost

TABLE 11

AVERAGE PUPIL-STAFF RATIO IN GRADES K TO 6 AND GRADES 7 TO 9 IN FIVE EASTERN STATES, BY STATES

| STATE | PUPIL-STAFF RATIO IN | | AMOUNT PUPIL-STAFF RATIO IN GRADES K–6 EXCEEDS PUPIL-STAFF RATIO IN GRADES 7–9 |
|---|---|---|---|
| | Grades K–6 | Grades 7–9 | |
| Connecticut | 27.7 | 23.9 | 3.8 |
| Massachusetts | 27.6 | 23.6 | 4.0 |
| New York | 24.3 | 19.8 | 4.5 |
| Pennsylvania | 31.0 | 24.0 | 7.0 |
| Rhode Island | 30.4 | 21.8 | 8.6 |
| Five States | 27.8 | 22.8 | 5.0 |

difference would be removed is made because the cost difference due to instructional salaries per pupil amounts to 75.4 per cent of the total cost difference in New York (see Table 10); hence to equalize both salaries and pupil-staff ratio in these two grade units will adjust 75.4 per cent of cost difference. However, the pupil-staff ratio affects costs other than instruction. It determines the entire cost difference in general control because, as has been explained, general control is allocated on the basis of the number of staff members in the elementary, junior high school, and senior high school units. It probably would affect costs in some other items such as operation and maintenance because to throw pupils into

TABLE 12

AVERAGE SALARIES PAID STAFF IN GRADES K TO 6 AND GRADES 7 TO 9 IN FIVE EASTERN STATES, BY STATES

| STATE | AVERAGE SALARY PAID IN | | AMOUNT AVERAGE SALARY PAID IN GRADES 7-9 EXCEEDS AVERAGE SALARY PAID IN GRADES K-6 |
| | Grades K-6 | Grades 7-9 | |
| --- | --- | --- | --- |
| Connecticut | $1,724.65 | $2,269.02 | $544.37 |
| Massachusetts | 1,697.19 | 1,926.04 | 228.85 |
| New York | 2,098.19 | 2,247.98 | 149.79 |
| Pennsylvania | 1,691.07 | 1,893.92 | 202.85 |
| Rhode Island | 1,459.77 | 1,727.43 | 267.66 |
| Five States | 1,765.84 | 1,997.61 | 231.77 |

larger groups would in the aggregate, although perhaps not in some individual cases, mean fewer rooms used and hence a smaller total expenditure for the same number of pupils. Therefore, if the pupil-staff ratio in the junior high school is adjusted to the pupil-staff ratio in the elementary school the effect would tend to equalize costs per pupil in some items other than instruction and, therefore, more than 75.4 per cent of the cost difference between the junior high school and the elementary units would be removed in New York. However, since the data as presented at this point are limited to instructional salaries only, the statements concerning the removal of cost differences are limited, in like manner, to the amounts involved in costs due to instructional salaries.

If, in the junior high schools of Rhode Island, there were, on the average, 8.6 more pupils per staff member and each staff member were paid $267.66 less salary than at present, instructional costs per pupil for salaries would be identical for elementary and junior high schools in the 6-3-3 systems of that state, and at least 75.9 per cent of the entire difference in costs per pupil between grades K to 6 and 7 to 9 would be removed.

Since New York and Rhode Island present the extreme cases among the five states in per pupil cost differences between the junior high school and the elementary units (see Table 4), it would be expected that these two states would present extreme cases in pupil-staff ratio differences and in salary differences. Tables 11 and 12 show that they do. That is, in New York, since the difference between the pupil-staff ratio in grades K to 6 and 7 to 9 is only 4.5 pupils per teacher and since the difference in average salaries between these two grade groups is only $149.79, the costs per pupil in the junior high school unit exceed the costs per pupil in the elementary unit by only 28.1 per cent (see Table 4). On the other hand, in Rhode Island the junior high school staff members average 8.6 fewer pupils than the elementary staff members and they receive a salary which averages $267.66 higher than that of grades K to 6. These two facts account largely for the high relative per pupil costs of grades 7 to 9, 61.5 per cent higher than those of grades K to 6.

Similar observations may be made for the other states. Massachusetts, which ranks low in comparative per pupil costs for the junior high school, also ranks low in difference in pupil-staff ratio (4.0), and low in difference in average salary paid ($228.85). Connecticut with its small pupil-staff ratio difference (3.8) shows a high relative per pupil cost in the junior high school because the difference in average salary paid is very large ($544.37). The reverse is true in Pennsylvania; the pupil-staff ratio difference is large (7.0) but the salary difference is small ($202.85).

When the five states are thrown together it may be said that if in the junior high schools there were, on the average, five more pupils per staff member and each staff member received $231.77 less salary than at present, the costs per pupil for instructional salaries would be identical in both elementary and junior high school units, and at least 74.7 per cent of the per pupil cost difference between these two grade groups would be removed.

When the one hundred seven 6–3–3 systems are classified by population groups rather than by states, the pupil-staff ratio and the average salaries paid in these groups are as indicated in Tables 13 and 14. Since there were no significant trends by population groups in the variations in per pupil costs between grades 7 to 9 and K to 6 (see Table 6), it might be expected that there would be no unusual trends shown by Tables 13 and 14. This appears to be true, but it would be possible for either salaries or pupil-staff ratio to be significantly more important in determining cost differ-

ences in one population group than in another. These tables
explain the low relative costs in grades 7 to 9 in the 10,000 to 30,000
group (see Table 6) by showing that there are only 3.9 fewer pupils
per staff member in the junior high school than in the elementary
and that the average salary paid in the former is only $186.14
higher than that paid in the latter. Similarly the other variations
in Table 6 may be explained largely in terms of the results shown in
Tables 13 and 14.

While this investigation was being carried on, the opinion was
often encountered that the teacher's salary was the one major item
which would account largely for higher costs in the junior high
school unit in the 6–3–3 systems. That, however, is not true of the
five states reported here. If it is assumed, for these five states,
that the present pupil-staff ratio in the junior high schools is maintained, but that the average junior high school salary is lowered to
the level of the average elementary salary, there would be a reduction of $231.77 per teacher for 5,274 teachers, or a total of

TABLE 13

AVERAGE PUPIL–STAFF RATIO IN GRADES K TO 6 AND IN GRADES 7 TO 9 IN
FIVE EASTERN STATES, BY POPULATION GROUPS

| POPULATION GROUP | PUPIL–STAFF RATIO IN | | AMOUNT PUPIL–STAFF RATIO IN GRADES K–6 EXCEEDS PUPIL–STAFF RATIO IN GRADES 7–9 |
|---|---|---|---|
| | Grades K–6 | Grades 7–9 | |
| More than 100,000 | 28.4 | 24.2 | 4.2 |
| 30,000–100,000 | 27.6 | 21.9 | 5.7 |
| 10,000–30,000 | 27.4 | 23.5 | 3.9 |
| 5,000–10,000 | 28.2 | 23.8 | 4.4 |
| All Groups | 27.8 | 22.8 | 5.0 |

TABLE 14

AVERAGE SALARIES PAID STAFF IN GRADES K TO 6 AND IN GRADES 7 TO 9
IN FIVE EASTERN STATES, BY POPULATION GROUPS

| POPULATION GROUP | AVERAGE SALARY PAID IN | | AMOUNT AVERAGE SALARY PAID IN GRADES 7–9 EXCEEDS AVERAGE SALARY PAID IN GRADES K–6 |
|---|---|---|---|
| | Grades K–6 | Grades 7–9 | |
| More than 100,000 | $1,811.67 | $2,086.12 | $274.45 |
| 30,000–100,000 | 1,805.15 | 2,041.79 | 236.64 |
| 10,000–30,000 | 1,643.99 | 1,830.13 | 186.14 |
| 5,000–10,000 | 1,584.53 | 1,832.36 | 247.83 |
| All Groups | 1,765.84 | 1,997.61 | 231.77 |

$1,222,354.98. This amounts to a reduction of $10.17 per pupil. If, on the other hand, it is assumed that junior high school salaries are held constant but that the number of staff members is reduced to the point where the junior high school pupil-staff ratio equals that of the elementary school, there will be 951 fewer staff members for the junior high schools of the five states. Since it is assumed that the junior high school salaries are held the same, the reduction in expenditures by this procedure will be the salaries of 951 staff members at $1,997.61 per teacher, or a total of $1,899,727.11. This reduces to $15.81 per pupil. Hence for these five states pupil-staff ratio is a much more important item than teachers' salaries in determining junior high school per pupil costs. Moreover, the influence of pupil-staff ratio on instructional salary costs per pupil only has been considered at this point. If the effects of the number of pupils per staff member on other items of cost were examined, it would be seen that pupil-staff ratio is even more influential in determining per pupil costs in the junior high school than has been indicated here.[6]

If the states are considered individually, it is found that in every one except Connecticut pupil-staff ratio is the most important item in determining the per pupil costs of junior high school education. The high relative costs in grades 7 to 9 in Rhode Island and in Pennsylvania may be explained largely in terms of pupil-staff ratio—8.6 fewer pupils per staff member in the junior high school unit than in the elementary school unit in Rhode Island, and 7 fewer pupils per staff member in the junior high school unit than in

[6]It should be understood that in this process of determining the relative importance of salaries and pupil-staff ratio, the two factors are not additive. That is, if the amount saved by reducing the number of staff members in the junior high school unit to a point where the pupil-staff ratio is the same as in the elementary school unit (but salaries in the junior high school are held the same) is added to the amount saved by reducing junior high school salaries to the elementary level (but pupil-staff ratio is held constant), this sum when subtracted from total junior high school expenditures will not yield a result which when divided by the number of pupils in average daily attendance in the junior high school will show a per pupil cost for instructional salaries the same as in the elementary school. This is due to the fact that even though both factors responsible for the difference in instructional costs are equalized, each is equalized when influenced by the other factor in the junior high school situation, and the latter is not comparable to the elementary situation. Pupil-staff ratio is equalized by reducing the number of staff members, but the number of staff members is multiplied by the junior high school salary rate. Likewise, when the salaries are equalized by being reduced to the elementary level the salary difference is multiplied by the number of staff members actually in the junior high school. Hence, whereas the results given here are correct for the conditions stated, they are not additive to account for the differences between junior high school and elementary school per pupil instructional costs. This could be accomplished by equalizing the salary rate and the pupil-staff ratio simultaneously, that is, in one operation, thus eliminating the junior high school effect entirely. Here, however, it is desired to measure the effect of each factor when the other factor is held in the junior high school situation.

the elementary school unit in Pennsylvania. These variations are considerably higher than those for the other states. However, the large variations in these two states are due not so much to a small pupil-staff ratio in grades 7 to 9 as to the large pupil-staff ratio in grades K to 6, each state averaging more than thirty pupils per staff member in the elementary unit.

It is apparent then that to explain much of the relatively higher per pupil costs of the junior high school unit one may look, in Connecticut, to teachers' salaries; in Rhode Island and Pennsylvania, to pupil-staff ratio; and in Massachusetts and New York, to both factors, although pupil-staff ratio is the major item in both of the latter states.

To show that the salaries paid and the number of pupils per staff member are by far the most important items in accounting for higher per pupil costs in grades 7 to 9 than in grades K to 6 does not complete the analysis of the situation. The examination should continue into every phase of junior high school education as distinguished from that of the lower grades to discover why, apparently, the former demands higher salaries and fewer pupils per staff member. Such an examination is to a large extent the subject matter of Chapter IX.

It was stated at the beginning of the chapter that there were three reasons for including this phase of the investigation: first, to report common practice in according financial support to grades 7 to 9 as opposed to grades K to 6 in 6–3–3 systems; second, to give certain reasons in explanation of cost variations between the junior high school unit and the elementary unit in 6–3–3 schools; and third, to offer some factual information relative to the common assumption that higher costs in grades 7 to 9 than in grades K to 6 in 6–3–3 systems establish higher costs for the junior high school unit than for the corresponding grades in the 8–4 type of organization. Evidence has been offered relative to the first two points. The third point, however, cannot be considered except in conjunction with the third phase of the investigation.

# VI

## Per Pupil Costs in the 6–3–3 and 8–4 Systems of Massachusetts

THE first phase, reported in the previous chapter, involves the issue of costs within the 6–3–3 type of organization only. The second phase, reported in this chapter, begins an examination of the cost of education in the junior high school organization as opposed to the traditional 8–4 organization. Specifically, it attempts to offer some evidence concerning per pupil costs in 6–3–3 systems as a whole in contrast with per pupil costs in 8–4 systems as a whole. Investigation concentrated upon those grades most directly involved in a shifting from one type of organization to another will probably yield more pertinent cost information than any other form of attack; a relevant issue, however, is the cost effect of reorganization on the entire system.

Arthur B. Lord, Supervisor of Educational Research and Statistics, Department of Education, Commonwealth of Massachusetts, stated to the investigator that it had long been his opinion that in Massachusetts, at least, the 6–3–3 systems as a whole were not costing more than the 8–4 systems of that state. Although he had worked out no specific cost data in support of his opinion, he felt that irrespective of the effect on per pupil costs in grades 7 to 9, changing from the 8–4 to the 6–3–3 type of organization in Massachusetts had not increased the per pupil costs in grades K to 12. Having just secured cost data from six states, including Massachusetts, which proved beyond question that grades 7 to 9 were costing considerably more than grades K to 6 in 6–3–3 systems, it seemed then to the investigator that, despite Mr. Lord's belief, the latter type of organization as a whole might show evidence of increased costs over the 8–4 type. This would necessarily be true unless the assumption were false that grades 7 to 9 in the junior high school cost more than these grades in the traditional school, or unless the 6–3–3 type of organization operated to lower costs in grades K to 6, or in grades 10 to 12.

Massachusetts was selected for this phase of the investigation from among the six eastern states included in the study because this state alone has established on a large scale the junior high school plan of education. To-day in the Massachusetts cities of more than 5,000 population, more pupils are enrolled in 6–3–3 systems than in any other one type of organization. Conditions in this state are probably due in no small degree to the attitude and efforts of the state department of education. Representative of the situation in Massachusetts is the following extract from a series of recommendations made by the state supervisors of elementary and secondary education to a local system of the state:

We are strongly of the opinion that a program for the expansion of school accommodations in Braintree [Massachusetts] should take into account the desirability of organizing the schools on the 6–3–3 basis. In very many of the most progressive school systems throughout the country, it has become the accepted practice to regard the elementary school as comprising grades one to six and the secondary school as comprising grades seven to twelve inclusive. . . . In most large towns and cities the secondary school division is sub-divided into the junior high school comprising grades seven, eight, and nine; and the senior high school comprising grades ten, eleven, and twelve. Ultimately, we believe that the secondary schools in Braintree should consist of two or three junior high schools and a senior high school.

It is unnecessary for us to elaborate at this point on the reasons for the widespread movement to organize the schools on the 6–3–3 basis. We believe it to be educationally sound as well as the most economical plan for providing all secondary school pupils with the variety of educational opportunities they should have. This movement has gone so far in Massachusetts that towns and cities involving more than one-half the population of the State are committed to this type of school organization.[1]

Massachusetts presents a clear-cut situation where the 6–3–3 type of organization has been established on such a wide scale and for such a period of time as to make the cost data from that state reflect a degree of representativeness, stability, and permanency which in all probability does not obtain in many other states.

The annual Report of the Department of Education of Massachusetts for the year ending November 30, 1931 (Tabulation of

[1]These recommendations were made by Supervisors B. F. Jones and F. P. Morse to H. D. Higgins, Chairman of the Braintree School Committee, on February 17, 1932. A copy was given to the investigator by C. Edward Fisher, Superintendent of Schools, Braintree, Massachusetts.

the School Returns, School Year Ending June 30, 1931, Part II)
lists 122 cities and towns of more than 5,000 population.

These are reported as organized on the following bases:

| | | |
|---|---|---|
| 8–4 plan | —— | 44 cities and towns |
| 6–3–3 plan | —— | 40 cities and towns |
| 6–2–4 plan | —— | 25 cities and towns |
| 6–3–3 plan (incomplete) | —— | 4 cities |
| 6–2–4 plan (incomplete) | —— | 1 city |
| 6–3–4 plan* | —— | 1 city |
| 8–5 plan | —— | 1 city |
| 7–2–3 plan | —— | 1 city and 1 town |
| 8 only | —— | 3 towns |
| 9–4 plan | —— | 1 town |

*Boston is reported as 6–3–4 by the Department of Education not because it has thirteen grades in
ts public school system but because it is a combination of 6–3–3 and 8–4.

Of the four cities incompletely organized on the 6–3–3 plan in
1930–1931, two, Fall River and New Bedford, made their financial
reports on the 6–3–3 basis and had so large a proportion of their
pupils in junior high schools that they are considered here as
being on the 6–3–3 plan, bringing the total of 6–3–3 systems of
more than 5,000 population up to forty-two. One of the two
remaining incomplete cities, Worcester, although making its
financial reports on the 6–3–3 basis, had so small a proportion of
the pupils in grades 7 to 9 enrolled in junior high schools that it is
not included in the 6–3–3 list. And since financial data were not
available on the 8–4 plan for Worcester it is impossible to include
the city in that group. Hence Worcester, like Boston, which
presents much the same situation, is not included in either the
6–3–3 or the 8–4 group. The fourth incomplete 6–3–3 city,
Newton, had few pupils in the junior high school and made its
financial report on the 8–4 basis; hence it is considered an 8–4
city here.

The incomplete 6–2–4 city, Brockton, since it was in fact an
8–4 system and made its financial report on that basis, is included
in the 8–4 group. The 8–5 system, Peabody, is in reality an 8–4
organization with one year of recognized graduate work. Since
practically all Massachusetts cities offer a year of graduate work
and, on the whole, report a considerable number of students, Peabody is included in the 8–4 list. These inclusions bring the list
of 8–4 cities and towns to forty-seven. Hence, of the 122 towns

and cities in Massachusetts of more than 5,000 population, forty-
two are classified as 6–3–3 systems, forty-seven as 8–4 systems,
and thirty-three are excluded because they cannot be classified
as either 6–3–3 or 8–4.   The majority of the schools excluded are
6–2–4 junior high schools.

In Table 15 the total costs, the total number of pupils in average daily attendance, and the costs per pupil in average daily
attendance are given by grade units for the forty-two Massachusetts 6–3–3 systems.   The same data for the forty-seven 8–4
systems are given in Table 16.   It is apparent at once that, taking
the school systems as a whole, the 250,202 pupils enrolled in the
6–3–3 organizations show a lower per pupil cost ($100.05) than the
155,625 pupils enrolled in the 8–4 organizations ($102.34).   This
definitely establishes at least one significant fact, namely, that in
Massachusetts in 1930–1931 those school systems in which the
grades were grouped on the 6–3–3 plan show a smaller per pupil
expenditure than those systems in which the grades were grouped
on the 8–4 plan.   This is particularly important relative to the
issue of the cost effects of grouping grades on a basis which varies
from the traditional plan.   What other implications there are
for junior high school education cannot be definitely stated, since
this study does not establish for these Massachusetts 6–3–3 systems
the provision or lack of provision for features of the reorganized
school other than that of grade grouping.   It may be that an examination would show as great a tendency in the 8–4 systems to
offer many of the features commonly considered peculiar to the
junior high school as would be found in the 6–3–3 systems.   While
this does not seem likely, the cost data here reported can be directly associated only with the method of grouping grades.

TABLE 15

TOTAL COSTS, TOTAL AVERAGE DAILY ATTENDANCE, AND COSTS PER PUPIL IN
AVERAGE DAILY ATTENDANCE FOR CURRENT EXPENSES IN GRADES K
TO 6, 7 TO 9, 10 TO 12, AND K TO 12 FOR FORTY-TWO
MASSACHUSETTS 6–3–3 SYSTEMS

| GRADE UNITS | TOTAL COST | A.D.A. | COSTS PER PUPIL IN A.D.A. |
|---|---|---|---|
| Grades K–6 | $13,062,841.50 | 154,495 | $ 84.55 |
| Grades 7–9 | 6,288,672.19 | 57,164 | 110.01 |
| Grades 10–12 | 5,682,076.06 | 38,543 | 147.42 |
| Grades K–12 | 25,033,589.75 | 250,202 | 100.05 |

Yet even if accurate information were at hand defining the educational programs of both the 6–3–3 and the 8–4 systems of Massachusetts, the problem would still be complex from the cost standpoint. It is complicated because, although the per pupil costs in grades K to 12 in 6–3–3 systems are slightly lower than in the 8–4 systems, the per pupil costs in grades 7 to 9 in the 6–3–3 systems are substantially higher than in grades K to 6 in these same systems. The explanation for this apparently lies in one or more of the following possibilities.

TABLE 16

TOTAL COSTS, TOTAL AVERAGE DAILY ATTENDANCE, AND COSTS PER PUPIL IN AVERAGE DAILY ATTENDANCE FOR CURRENT EXPENSES IN GRADES K TO 8, 9 TO 12, AND K TO 12 FOR FORTY–SEVEN MASSACHUSETTS 8–4 SYSTEMS

| Grade Units | Total Cost | A.D.A. | Costs per Pupil in A.D.A. |
|---|---|---|---|
| Grades K–8 | $10,840,412.02 | 117,792 | $ 92.03 |
| Grades 9–12 | 5,083,772.08 | 37,833 | 134.37 |
| Grades K–12 | 15,924,184.10 | 155,625 | 102.34 |

First, it may be that, by chance or because of some unknown selective factor, the 6–3–3 communities tend to accord somewhat less financial support to their schools as a whole, but that because grades 7 to 9 cost relatively more in the 6–3–3 systems than in the 8–4, costs in grades K to 12 in the 6–3–3 systems are therefore raised to a level which is almost as high as in the 8–4 systems. That is, these 6–3–3 systems might show materially lower costs than they now show if they were 8–4 systems; perhaps the only reason they exhibit costs which approach those of the 8–4 systems is that the presence of the junior high school grades tends to raise the whole level of costs.

Second, it may be that the 6–3–3 type of organization operates to lower costs in the grades below or above the junior high school unit. That is, higher costs in grades 7 to 9 might be offset by lower costs in grades K to 6 or grades 10 to 12 to such an extent that costs in grades K to 12 in 6–3–3 systems would not differ materially from those in 8–4.

Third, it may be that in the 6–3–3 and 8–4 systems of Massachusetts per pupil costs are similar not only in grades K to 12 but also in grades K to 6, 7 to 9, and 10 to 12. That is, the explanation of similar costs in grades K to 12 for the two types of organization may lie in similar costs in grades 7 to 9, rather than in higher costs in grades 7 to 9 in 6–3–3 systems balanced by lower costs in grades K to 6 or 10 to 12. If this is true costs must be materially higher in grades 7 to 9 than in K to 6 in 8–4 as well as in 6–3–3 systems.

The only way to secure a complete answer to the above issues is to segregate the costs in grades 7 and 8 from those in grades K to 8 and the costs in grade 9 from those in grades 9 to 12 in the forty-seven 8–4 systems. This is a task of such magnitude as to be not feasible in this study. Nevertheless, certain other evidence is available, and each of the three possible explanations of the Massachusetts cost data is given brief examination below.

While great reliance should not be placed upon a direct comparison of costs, there appears to be nothing to indicate that in the 8–4 systems of Massachusetts grades K to 6 and 10 to 12 should be accorded a higher level of support than these grades in the 6–3–3 organizations. On the whole the forty-two 6–3–3 systems seem comparable to the forty-seven 8–4 systems; both types of organization operate side by side in the Metropolitan area around Boston and in the less urban communities of the western part of the state. The two wealthy 8–4 cities of Cambridge and Brookline are balanced by the fact that many of the poorer mill cities of Massachusetts are also 8–4 organizations. Table 17 gives the

TABLE 17

TOTAL PROPERTY VALUATION, TOTAL AVERAGE DAILY ATTENDANCE, AND VALUATION PER PUPIL IN AVERAGE DAILY ATTENDANCE FOR FORTY-TWO MASSACHUSETTS 6–3–3 SYSTEMS AND FORTY–SEVEN MASSACHUSETTS 8–4 SYSTEMS, BY TYPE OF ORGANIZATION

| Type of Organization | Total Valuation as of April 1, 1930 | Total A.D.A. | Valuation per Pupil in A.D.A. |
|---|---|---|---|
| 6–3–3 | $2,390,519,588.00 | 250,202 | $ 9,554.36 |
| 8–4 | 1,563,433,635.00 | 155,625 | 10,046.16 |

property valuation per pupil in average daily attendance for the two groups of systems. In so far as assessed valuation and geographical location are indicative of comparability these two groups are reasonably alike.

To support the contention that some of the grades other than

7 to 9 are accorded greater financial support in the 8–4 systems than in the 6–3–3 systems, it might be pointed out that per pupil costs in grades K to 8 in the former organizations are $92.03 whereas in grades K to 6 in the latter systems they are only $84.55 (see Tables 15 and 16).   However, these two grade units do not correspond; higher costs in grades 7 and 8 in the 8–4 systems might well account for higher costs in grades K to 8.   Moreover, costs per pupil are substantially lower in grades 9 to 12 in the 8–4 organizations than in grades 10 to 12 in the 6–3–3 systems, $134.37 compared with $147.42.

The second possible interpretation of the Massachusetts cost data was that grades 7 to 9 in the 6–3–3 systems might show substantially higher costs than these same grades in the 8–4 systems, but that the 6–3–3 type of organization might operate to lower costs in grades K to 6 or grades 10 to 12.   This would account for the approximately equal expenditures for all the grades combined, in the two types of organization.   Reference to Tables 15 and 16 shows that this might be true since per pupil costs in grades K to 6 in the 6–3–3 systems not only are substantially lower than per pupil costs in grades 7 to 9 in the same systems but also are lower than per pupil costs in grades K to 8 in the 8–4 systems.   However, little reliance may be placed upon a comparison of two grade groups which are not corresponding units. Moreover, as has already been stated in Chapter III, an attempt was made to discover whether shifting to the 6–3–3 type of organization had any significant cost effects on grades K to 6.   It was discovered that reorganization in no case materially affected these costs.   The same salary schedule remained in effect and the educational program was left unchanged.   Except that in some instances grades K to 6 occupied an entire building which before reorganization housed grades K to 8 no evidence was discovered which pointed to any change in per pupil costs in grades K to 6 after the adoption of the junior high school plan.   In several cases enough financial data were at hand to make possible a comparison of costs in grades K to 8 before reorganization with costs in grades K to 6 after reorganization.[2]   In each case the former costs were substantially higher than the latter.   This at first was

[2]While it is believed that the data upon which these statements are based were reasonably reliable it is not possible to state positively that they were since systems during the period of reorganization, which often lasts several years, may make changes which cannot be associated with the reorganization movement.

interpreted as a strong indication that the junior high school organization operated in these systems to lower elementary costs. However, continued examination disclosed no appreciable changes in personnel and no changes whatsoever in salaries or program of education, but did disclose certain evidence pointing to higher costs in grades 7 and 8 than in grades K to 6 before reorganization. It was finally concluded, therefore, that costs in grades K to 6 were less after reorganization than were costs in grades K to 8 before the change because grades K to 6 under the new plan were relieved of the cost effect of grades 7 and 8.

The possible cost effects of reorganization on grades 10 to 12 appear to be more complex. When reorganization takes place, the regular four-year high school is often materially affected. There is some shifting of teachers, and sometimes the program of studies is changed to make possible a continuation of the work provided by the enriched and broadened curricula of the junior high school unit. In the few cases where financial figures were available it was found that per pupil costs in grades 10 to 12 were always somewhat higher after reorganization than the per pupil costs in grades 9 to 12 before the change. This might indicate a tendency toward higher costs in the senior high school than in the regular four-year high school. However, as the investigation progressed the data pointed in another direction, namely, that costs in grade 9 were almost invariably lower than costs in grades 10 to 12 in regular four-year high schools and that higher costs in grades 10 to 12 in the senior high school could largely be explained by the fact that these grades after reorganization merely reflected what the true costs would have shown had they been segregated from grade 9 before reorganization.

Data which bear directly upon the question of costs in grade 9 as distinguished from costs in grades 10 to 12 in 8–4 systems are introduced in Chapter VII (see Tables 27 and 28). Since these data show per pupil costs in grade 9 to be consistently and substantially lower than per pupil costs in grades 10 to 12 in 8–4 systems, they lend considerable weight to the belief that higher costs in grades 10 to 12 after reorganization are due largely to the absence of grade 9. However, further investigation should be made of the cost effect of the 6–3–3 type of organization on grades 10 to 12, particularly as it relates to changes in the program of studies and the cost implications of such changes.

To explain the Massachusetts financial data showing higher costs in grades K to 12 in 8–4 systems than in 6–3–3 two possibilities have been offered. A third explanation might be that costs in grades 7 to 9 in the 6–3–3 systems do not differ materially from costs in grades 7 to 9 in 8–4 systems. That is, instead of clinging tenaciously to the proposition that costs in grades 7 to 9 must be relatively higher in 6–3–3 systems than in 8–4 systems and then seeking hidden causes to explain equal costs in grades K to 12 in the two types of organization—such as higher relative costs in grades 7 to 9, accompanied by lower relative costs in grades K to 6 or 10 to 12—the argument is advanced that perhaps, in these two groups of Massachusetts systems which show almost identical costs in grades K to 12, the costs in grades K to 6, 7 to 9, and 10 to 12 are likewise almost identical for the two groups of systems. To prove conclusively that this is true or that it is untrue would require a segregation of costs in the 8–4 systems— grades 7 and 8 from grades K to 8 and grade 9 from grades 9 to 12. That, however, is not feasible for forty-seven systems.

Another method of comparison is that of making the grade units in the 6–3–3 organizations comparable to those in the 8–4 organizations. This may be done by assuming that the per pupil costs in grades 7 to 9 in the 6–3–3 systems average the same for each of the grades in this unit. When such an assumption is made the costs in grades 7 and 8 may readily be segregated from those in grades 7 to 9, and with the costs so segregated those in grades 7 and 8 may be combined with grades K to 6 and those in grade 9 may be combined with grades 10 to 12. Such a procedure will make 6–3–3 costs available on the 8–4 plan of grade grouping. When this is done for the forty-two Massachusetts 6–3–3 systems the results are as indicated in Table 18. As would be expected this procedure results in raising the costs in grades K to 8 to a level somewhat above that of costs in grades K to 6, $89.69 compared with $84.55, and in lowering the costs in grades 9 to 12 to a point somewhat below that of costs in grades 10 to 12, $135.49 compared with $147.42.

When a direct comparison of per pupil costs in grades K to 8, 9 to 12, and K to 12 in the forty-two 6–3–3 systems is made with these same grade units in the forty-seven 8–4 systems, the results are as shown in Table 19. This table shows only slight variations for each of the grade groups. While the results exhibited here

TABLE 18

TOTAL COSTS, TOTAL AVERAGE DAILY ATTENDANCE, AND COSTS PER PUPIL IN
AVERAGE DAILY ATTENDANCE FOR FORTY–TWO MASSACHUSETTS 6–3–3
SYSTEMS, DIVIDED ON THE 8–4 BASIS*

| Grade Unit | Total Cost | A.D.A. | Cost per Pupil in A.D.A. |
|---|---|---|---|
| Grades K–8 | $17,365,283.14 | 193,604 | $ 89.69 |
| Grades 9–12 | 7,668,306.61 | 56,598 | 135.49 |
| Grades K–12 | 25,033,589.75 | 250,202 | 100.05 |

*Grades 7 and 8 are combined with grades K to 6 and grade 9 is combined with grades 10 to 12
on the assumption that per pupil costs are the same for grades 7, 8, and 9.

TABLE 19

COSTS PER PUPIL IN AVERAGE DAILY ATTENDANCE IN GRADES K TO 8, 9 TO 12,
AND K TO 12 FOR FORTY–TWO MASSACHUSETTS 6–3–3 SYSTEMS AND
FORTY–SEVEN MASSACHUSETTS 8–4 SYSTEMS, BY TYPE
OF ORGANIZATION

| Type of Organization | Cost per Pupil | | |
|---|---|---|---|
| | Grades K–8 | Grades 9–12 | Grades K–12 |
| 6–3–3 | $89.69 | $135.49 | $100.05 |
| 8–4 | 92.03 | 134.37 | 102.34 |

do not offer conclusive evidence on all of the issues raised in this
chapter they do establish beyond question that not only do grades
K to 12 show a slightly lower cost in the 6–3–3 systems of Massachusetts than in the 8–4 organizations, but that likewise grades
K to 8 show a lower cost in the junior high school organizations
than in the traditional systems. On the other hand per pupil
costs in grades 9 to 12 are slightly higher in the reorganized schools
than in the unreorganized. Perhaps the most significant thing
is that such close similarity should be shown between the two
types of organization for each of the groups of grades.[3]

[3]The calculation in the above direct comparison of per pupil costs in grades K to 8 in the two
types of organization in Massachusetts is, as was indicated, based upon the assumption that per pupil
costs averaged the same for grades 7, 8, and 9. Such an assumption may have introduced a slight
error into cost figures for grades 7 and 8 in the 6–3–3 systems. However, the amount to which this assumption will throw the calculation into error, while not large, will be in the direction of showing
higher costs for grades 7 and 8 in the 6–3–3 cities than actually exist because grade 9 will probably show
a slightly higher cost than grades 7 and 8. Hence, the costs in grades 7 and 8 charged to these grades
in the Massachusetts 6–3–3 schools may be a little too high, and the statement that grades K to 8 in
the 6–3–3 schools show a lower cost than these same grades in the 8–4 schools would undoubtedly be
reinforced by the cost findings if it were possible to offer actual instead of computed costs here.

The results exhibited in Table 19, since they are based on the 8–4 rather than on the 6–3–3 plan, fail to indicate one important item, namely, whether the $92.03 per pupil cost in grades K to 8 in the 8–4 systems is uniform for grades K to 8, or whether grades K to 6 would show a lower and grades 7 and 8 a higher per pupil cost if the costs for these two grade groups were segregated. Although the results in this table do not prove the situation one way or another, they do add weight to the belief that grades 7 and 8 in 8–4 systems probably are accorded a somewhat higher level of financial support than the grades below. If they are not, then grades K to 6 in the 8–4 systems of Massachusetts must cost substantially more than grades K to 6 in the 6–3–3 systems, which does not seem likely.

The same reasoning may be applied to grades 9 to 12. These grades show almost identical costs in both types of organization, $135.49 in the 6–3–3 systems and $134.37 in the 8–4. Yet the senior high school grades show a cost of $147.42 as opposed to $134.37 in the regular high school. Either grades 10 to 12 in the 6–3–3 systems cost considerably more than these same grades in the 8–4 systems, or in the latter systems grade 9 carries a lower cost than grades 10 to 12.

It does not seem likely that the 6–3–3 systems of Massachusetts support grades K to 6 on a level substantially lower, and grades 10 to 12 on a level substantially higher than do the 8–4 systems, although costs in grades 7 to 9 in the two types of organization might thereby be equalized. It seems more likely that in these two large and reasonably comparable groups of Massachusetts systems grades K to 6 and grades 10 to 12 would be accorded somewhat similar financial support. If this is true, then grades 7 to 9 in both groups show approximately the same costs, and in the 8–4 systems grades 7 and 8 carry higher costs than grades K to 6. The almost identical costs in grades K to 8, 9 to 12, and K to 12 for the two types of organization do not prove this to be true but they give some reason for such a belief. However, more conclusive proof is possible only when there is a segregation of costs in grades 7 and 8 from costs in grades K to 8, and a segregation of costs in grade 9 from costs in grades 9 to 12 in 8–4 systems. The results of such a segregation are reported in the next two chapters.

If it is true that in these two large groups of Massachusetts school systems the per pupil costs in grades 7 to 9 are approximately the same, both actually and relatively (that is, relative to costs in grades K to 6), then cost conditions in this respect are somewhat contrary to a considerable body of opinion. In searching for the elements or causes which might explain such a situation, the investigator kept in mind that the two major factors contributing to differences in cost between grades K to 6 and grades 7 to 9 in 6–3–3 systems were salaries paid the instructional staff and the number of pupils per staff member. It seemed likely that these two factors might be equally important in explaining similarities or dissimilarities in per pupil costs between grades 7 to 9 and K to 6 in 8–4 systems. However, data bearing directly upon salaries and pupil-staff ratio in grades 7 to 9 as a distinct unit in 8–4 systems were no more available than were data relative to per pupil costs. But other data were available, the proportion of pupils in grades 7 and 8 to those in grades K to 6 in both 6 3 3 and 8–4 organizations. It is believed that these data are important in connection with the tendency to maintain the same number of classes in the upper grades as in the lower, even though the enrollment usually falls off somewhat in the former.

In cities of all sizes elementary schools are often small. In these smaller schools when the enrollment in the first grade is sufficient for only one, two, or three teachers, it is often difficult or impossible to have less than the same number of teachers in the upper grades, because the enrollment, although usually less in the upper grades than in the lower, is not sufficiently less to make possible the dropping of a teacher. For this reason, as well as for others, one will often find smaller classes in grades 7 and 8 than in grades 1 to 6. If this operates to a substantial extent in 8–4 systems it will lend weight to the belief that per pupil costs in grades 7 and 8 are higher than in grades K to 6 and therefore perhaps relatively similar to per pupil costs in grades 7 and 8 in 6–3–3 systems.

The total membership[4] on October 1, 1930 in grades 1 to 6, 7 and 8, 9, 7 to 9, and 10 to 12 for the forty-two 6–3–3 systems and the forty-seven 8–4 systems of Massachusetts is given in

---

[4]Membership was used in place of A.D.A. because of the nature of the attendance records in Massachusetts. A.D.A. is, of course, reported in Massachusetts but membership is more readily computed for isolated grades. Kindergarten membership is not included in grades 1 to 6.

Table 20. Since relative membership is not readily seen in Table 20 the data in that table are reproduced as relative figures in Table 21. This table indicates that for every 100 pupils in grades 1 to 6 in the 6–3–3 schools of Massachusetts on October 1, 1930, there were 29.7 pupils in grades 7 and 8, 13.7 in grade 9, 43.4

TABLE 20

MEMBERSHIP IN GRADES 1 TO 6, 7 AND 8, 9, 7 TO 9, AND 10 TO 12 FOR FORTY–TWO
MASSACHUSETTS 6–3–3 SYSTEMS AND FORTY–SEVEN MASSACHUSETTS 8–4
SYSTEMS, BY TYPE OF ORGANIZATION
October 1, 1930

| TYPE OF ORGANIZATION | MEMBERSHIP | | | | |
| --- | --- | --- | --- | --- | --- |
| | Grades 1–6 | Grades 7–8 | Grade 9 | Grades 7–9 | Grades 10–12 |
| 6–3–3 | 150,626 | 44,796 | 20,636 | 65,432 | 41,187 |
| 8–4 | 93,010 | 27,487 | 13,369 | 40,856 | 28,506 |

TABLE 21

RELATIVE MEMBERSHIP IN GRADES 1 TO 6, 7 AND 8, 9, 7 TO 9, AND 10 TO 12 FOR
FORTY–TWO MASSACHUSETTS 6–3–3 SYSTEMS AND FORTY–SEVEN
MASSACHUSETTS 8–4 SYSTEMS, BY TYPE OF ORGANIZATION
October 1, 1930

| TYPE OF ORGANIZATION | RATIO OF MEMBERSHIP WHEN MEMBERSHIP IN GRADES 1 TO 6 EQUALS 100 | | | | |
| --- | --- | --- | --- | --- | --- |
| | Grades 1–6 | Grades 7–8 | Grade 9 | Grades 7–9 | Grades* 10–12 |
| 6–3–3 | 100 | 29.7 | 13.7 | 43.4 | 27.3 |
| 8–4 | 100 | 29.5 | 14.4 | 43.9 | 30.6 |

*These grades include, for both types of organization, so-called grade 13 or post-graduate grade of the high school.

in grades 7 to 9, and 27.3 in grades 10 to 12. Likewise, for every 100 pupils in grades 1 to 6 in the 8–4 schools there were 29.5 pupils in grades 7 and 8, 14.4 in grade 9, 43.9 in grades 7 to 9, and 30.6 in grades 10 to 12.

The proportion of pupils in grades 7 and 8 is practically the same in both types of organization, being a fraction of a per cent higher in the 6–3–3 systems, 29.7 compared with 29.5 in the traditional organizations. Hence, as between types of organization there appears to be no appreciable difference in Massachusetts, for this particular year, in the falling off in enrollment in the upper grades.

However, the important thing is not that the two types of organization show a similar falling off in enrollment, since this decline may not affect the reorganized school in the same manner that it affects the traditional school,[5] but the amount of the decline in the 8–4 systems.   If it is assumed that the 93,010 pupils in grades 1 to 6 in the 8–4 systems are evenly distributed through these six grades there will be approximately 15,501 pupils in each grade.   If these 15,501 pupils in each grade are divided into classes or teaching units of 30 each there will be approximately 517 teaching units per grade.   Assuming further that the 27,487 pupils in grades 7 and 8 in the 8–4 systems are evenly divided between these two grades there will be 13,743 pupils in each grade. If the 517 teaching units in grades 1 to 6 are continued through grades 7 and 8 there will be not 30 pupils per class, but only 26.6 pupils (13,743 divided by 517).   A falling off of only 3.4 pupils in a class of 30 seems relatively small.   Yet in terms of per pupil costs it is substantial, as may be seen from the effects of pupil-staff ratio differences on per pupil costs as indicated in Chapter V. The difference in class size shown above as being a possible result of a decline in enrollment in the upper grades in the 8–4 systems in Massachusetts is not greatly less than the pupil-staff ratio difference between grades K to 6 and grades 7 to 9 in the 6–3–3 systems in this state (see Table 11).   However, it is not assumed that all of the decline in enrollment in the upper grades is translated into smaller classes; there is often a reduction in teaching units in these upper grades.

Nevertheless, common practice which seems to incline toward a continuation of the same number of classes in the upper grades, particularly in the smaller systems, indicates that a substantial decline in enrollment may be one of the major factors in explaining pupil-teacher or pupil-staff differences between grades K to 6 and grades 7 and 8 in 8–4 systems, and may likewise indicate higher per pupil costs in grades 7 and 8 than in grades K to 6 in the traditional systems of Massachusetts.   It appears then that, whereas certain features of the junior high school may tend to cause smaller classes in grades 7 and 8, the reorganized school has one distinct advantage over the traditional school, namely,

---

[5]In most cases the elementary pupils from more than one building are concentrated in one junior high school.   Hence there would be an opportunity to start all first year junior high school classes at or near a maximum size.

in those cases where junior high school pupils are well concentrated there is little administrative difficulty in starting all classes
at a maximum.

Because the data in Tables 20 and 21 are for one year only it
was thought advisable to secure similar data for another year.
The total membership on October 1, 1931 in grades 1 to 6, 7 and 8,
9, 7 to 9, and 10 to 12 in the forty-two 6–3–3 and the forty-seven
8–4 systems of Massachusetts is given in Table 22.   The year

TABLE 22

MEMBERSHIP IN GRADES 1 TO 6, 7 AND 8, 9, 7 TO 9, AND 10 TO 12 FOR FORTY–TWO
MASSACHUSETTS 6–3–3 SYSTEMS AND FORTY–SEVEN MASSACHUSETTS 8–4
SYSTEMS, BY TYPE OF ORGANIZATION
October 1, 1931

| TYPE OF ORGANIZATION | MEMBERSHIP | | | | |
|---|---|---|---|---|---|
| | Grades 1–6 | Grades 7–8 | Grade 9 | Grades 7–9 | Grades 10–12 |
| 6–3–3 | 153,002 | 45,088 | 24,674 | 69,762 | 45,473 |
| 8–4 | 93,713 | 27,898 | 14,635 | 42,533 | 29,702 |

TABLE 23

RELATIVE MEMBERSHIP IN GRADES 1 TO 6, 7 AND 8, 9, 7 TO 9, AND 10 TO 12 FOR
FORTY–TWO MASSACHUSETTS 6–3–3 SYSTEMS AND FORTY–SEVEN
MASSACHUSETTS 8–4 SYSTEMS, BY TYPE OF ORGANIZATION
October 1, 1931

| TYPE OF ORGANIZATION | RATIO OF MEMBERSHIP WHEN MEMBERSHIP IN GRADES 1 TO 6 EQUALS 100 | | | | |
|---|---|---|---|---|---|
| | Grades 1–6 | Grades 7–8 | Grade 9 | Grades 7–9 | Grades* 10–12 |
| 6–3–3 | 100 | 29.4 | 16.1 | 45.6 | 29.7 |
| 8–4 | 100 | 29.8 | 15.6 | 45.4 | 31.7 |

*These grades include, for both types of organization, so-called grade 13 or post-graduate grade of
the high school.

1931 shows an increase in membership over 1930 for both types
of organization in all groups of grades, but the increase is greater
in the 6–3–3 systems in every grade group.   Table 23 gives the
October 1, 1931 membership in relative form.   Tables 21 and 23
show an almost identical relationship between the numbers in
grades 1 to 6 and grades 7 and 8 for 1930 and 1931.   Hence from
the standpoint of the decline in the upper grades the increased
enrollment in 1931 over 1930 has made no appreciable change.

A comparison of Tables 21 and 23 is interesting for another reason. For the year 1930 the enrollment in grade 9 was 13.7 per cent of the enrollment in grades 1 to 6 in the 6–3–3 systems and 14.4 per cent in the 8–4 systems, but in 1931 this per cent had increased to 16.1 in the 6–3–3 systems and to 15.6 in the 8–4 systems. While this is a substantial increase for both types of organization it is particularly large in the 6–3–3 systems, an increase from 13.7 to 16.1 pupils in grade 9 for every 100 pupils in grades 1 to 6. Since, however, this increase is so substantial, showing as it does a figure for grade 9 which is more than half that of grades 7 and 8 (16.1 is appreciably more than 14.7, half of 29.4, the per cent for grades 7 and 8 combined), it is probable that the increasing tendency of small eight-year schools to send pupils out of their districts for high school work is noticeable here. Moreover, too much faith should not be placed in the trends shown by a comparison of but two years.

For grades 10 to 12 the 8–4 systems show a gain of 1.1 pupils for every 100 in grades 1 to 6, and the 6–3–3 systems show a gain of 2.4 pupils. If the change from 1930 to 1931 is more than mere chance and is indicative of a definite trend, it would appear that for grade 9 and grades 10 to 12 the 6–3–3 systems are increasing their holding power. Whether or not this is true, the relationship at the present time between membership in the lower and the upper grades in both types of organization indicates that their holding power is quite similar and hence insofar as the retention of pupils is a factor in total costs there seems to be little difference between the two types of organization.

This chapter has introduced certain data to show that per pupil costs in grades K to 8, grades 9 to 12, and, therefore, also in grades K to 12 are approximately the same in the 6–3–3 and 8–4 systems of Massachusetts cities of more than 5,000 total population. It has introduced certain other data which seem to indicate that per pupil costs in grades 7 to 9 are likewise similar in the two types of organization. More conclusive evidence relative to this latter point is offered in the next chapter.

# VII

# Per Pupil Costs in Grades 7 to 9 in the 6–3–3 and 8–4 Types of Organization

THE first phase of this investigation dealt with per pupil costs in the 6–3–3 type of organization only; the second phase was extended to include certain aspects of per pupil costs in grades K to 8, 9 to 12, and K to 12 in both 6–3–3 and 8–4 systems. This third phase is a more intensive study of the cost effect of type of organization on grades 7 to 9. The indirect method of cost comparison employed in this third phase is described in Chapter III, and the manner of securing the data is given in some detail in Chapter IV.

As was stated in the latter chapter it was found necessary to limit the number of systems from which to draw data for this part of the study to twenty-four—twelve 6–3–3 and twelve 8–4 systems—because of the detailed work required in this phase of the investigation, particularly in securing cost data in grades 7 to 9 in the 8–4 organizations.

The twelve 6–3–3 systems were selected first. They were chosen from among the one hundred seven 6–3–3 systems reported in the first phase of this investigation on the several bases indicated below.

*Enrollment.*—They were selected to represent a wide range of enrollment, much the same as that of the 107 systems.

*Types of Communities.*—An attempt was made to select organizations that are located in various types of communities, industrial, residential, agricultural, urban, and rural.

*Wealth.*—The systems represent school districts which vary from those showing a high per pupil wealth to those showing a comparatively low per pupil wealth.

*Geographical Areas.*—Although there was some tendency to select systems readily reached from New York City, the systems are located in three states, six of them representing all sections of Massachusetts.

*Type of Organization.*—No system was selected unless it represented a completed 6–3–3 organization, that is, one in which all pupils in grades 7 to 9 are enrolled in a separately organized junior high school unit and in which all elementary and senior high school pupils are enrolled in separately organized units of grades K to 6 or 1 to 6, and 10 to 12 respectively. Only those systems were chosen which were fully recognized as 6–3–3 institutions by the department of education of the state in which they were located.

*Educational Program.*—It has already been indicated that the first three phases of this study deal largely with the question of costs in the 6–3–3 type of organization as such systems actually function in the East to-day, with but little reference to the type of educational program offered.[1] Such a limitation of the study seems deliberately to reject that which may constitute the major aspect of the junior high school from the cost standpoint—the program of education provided. That is, as has so often been pointed out by those familiar with junior high school education, the mere regrouping of grades on a three unit basis, as the 6–3–3 or 6–2–4 plan, is no guarantee that such a system offers the other features of the reorganized school. Hence the problem presented itself at this point as to whether or not the twelve systems chosen were to be selected on the further basis of type of educational program, that is, whether or not only systems which satisfied every feature of the ideal junior high school would be acceptable. For several reasons the decision was reached that this would not be made a major test.

First, it was discovered during this investigation that the one feature of the junior high school which is looked upon by the average community as primary and as the one most associated with costs is the method of grouping grades. Apparently, therefore, irrespective of the fact that the actual program of studies may be more far-reaching in its effect on costs, the data most needed at present concern the cost effects of the regrouping of grades, regardless of educational program. It is the establishment of this new unit of grades which appears as the unknown step to so many communities which take reorganization under consideration.

Second, while standard or ideal junior high school education has been well defined and described in terms of general features, there is less common agreement about specific ways and means of at-

[1] See Chapter III.

taining these features. For example, recognition of individual differences is almost universally accepted as essential to standard junior high school education. Yet the means of recognizing these differences vary widely both in theory and in practice. Not only is the question of how best to provide for individual differences unsettled, but there are other controversial issues, since the standard junior high school comprehends much of what is called progressive education. Hence, to provide a general check-list of junior high school features and to make selections of systems on such bases would prove almost futile. To prepare a detailed check-list would be to set up an outline of features as extensive as that which serves as the basis of such comprehensive treatments of the junior high school as those of Briggs, Koos, and Smith.

Third, the last phase of the investigation is to be given entirely to a discussion of the cost implications of the features of the standard junior high school; hence emphasis upon type of organization in these first three phases does not operate to exclude completely the cost issues involved in the ideal junior high school program of education.

While no attempt was made to select only those 6–3–3 systems which in every way appeared to provide the features of the standard junior high school, no systems were selected which obviously failed to provide such features; hence the twelve systems finally chosen probably represent a type of junior high school education which is more progressive than that of many 6–3–3 systems.

After the 6–3–3 systems had been chosen—but before there had been any investigation of their costs—the twelve 8–4 systems were selected. The latter systems were chosen primarily not because it was believed that they were representative of the whole group of 8–4 systems in communities of more than 5,000 population, but because they were at least somewhat comparable to the 6–3–3 group in such matters as population, average daily attendance, type of community, wealth per pupil, and diversity of geographical location. In order to assure a reasonable degree of comparability between the two groups there was selected for each of the twelve 6–3–3 systems a corresponding 8–4 system; that is, it was believed that the best method of securing two groups which would be similar as a whole would be to select systems which balanced each other in pairs. For example, Hartford, Connecticut, was selected as an 8–4 system to correspond to the largest of the 6–3–3 systems,

Springfield, Massachusetts. Likewise, in the smaller population group, Brookline, Massachusetts, was picked to balance White Plains, New York; and the 8–4 system, Clinton, Massachusetts, was chosen to correspond to the smallest 6–3–3 community, Adams, Massachusetts.

However, while an attempt was made to pair each 6–3–3 system with a comparable 8–4 system, such extreme care and caution were not exercised as would have been necessary were a direct comparison of costs to have been made. It should be recalled at this point that the per pupil costs in grades 7 to 9 in each system of each type of organization are to be related to the per pupil costs in grades K to 6 in the same system, and that only this ratio of costs within the system is utilized in making comparisons between different types of organization. This indirect method of cost comparison is employed, as has been explained in some detail, because of the impossibility of selecting two perfectly comparable groups of systems. Moreover, in this investigation little reliance is placed upon any results obtained by contrasting one 6–3–3 system with its corresponding 8–4 system; significance will be attached, however, to the results of each group as a whole and to definite tendencies within the group.

The problem of the type of educational program provided, which was encountered in the selection of the 6–3–3 systems, was likewise encountered in the selection of the 8–4 systems. Just as 6–3–3 systems are not all standard junior high schools, 8–4 systems do not all provide conservative programs of education. Again, it was decided that the features of traditional education other than organization of grades on the 8–4 plan would not be given primary consideration. A survey of the field will show few 8–4 systems in centers of more than 5,000 population which do not provide some features usually associated with the reorganized school, such as departmentalization, recognition of individual differences, and some attempt at guidance. Hence, systems were selected which present a variety of 8–4 administrative features as well as a variety of educational programs.[2]

Certain elements of this situation should be stressed. While the twelve 6–3–3 systems were selected as representative of a consider-

[2]Hartford, Connecticut, has the district system for the control of elementary schools. Passaic, New Jersey, is partly organized on the platoon basis. Several systems show a tendency to house some of the upper grade pupils in units which are distinct from the lower grades.

able range of population, wealth, type of community, and geographical area, it is not known that these twelve systems constitute an adequate sampling of the 6–3–3 type of junior high school in the six eastern states. It is believed that they are fairly representative. However, the conclusions reached are claimed for these twelve systems only. Further, the twelve 8–4 systems were chosen because they show a fair degree of comparability with the 6–3–3 systems; although, representing as they do a considerable range in a variety of factors, they should be somewhat representative of 8–4 systems in general. From an indirect comparison of the per pupil costs in these two groups, such as has been explained, it is believed that light may be thrown upon the issue of the financial consequences of grades 7 to 9 organized as a separate unit in a junior high school system in contrast to these grades when organized as in the traditional school. Finally, it should be understood that the primary purpose here is to measure a type of organization and not a program of education, although the 6–3–3 organizations tend to provide the more progressive features of education and the 8–4 organizations on the whole are somewhat more conservative.

The twenty-four selected systems together with their average daily attendance in grades K to 12 and grades 7 to 9, and the total city population in each community are given in Table 24. In this

TABLE 24

PUPILS IN AVERAGE DAILY ATTENDANCE, GRADES K TO 12 AND GRADES 7 TO 9, AND TOTAL POPULATION, TWELVE SELECTED 6–3–3 SYSTEMS AND TWELVE SELECTED 8–4 SYSTEMS

| 6–3–3 SYSTEMS | | | | 8–4 SYSTEMS | | | |
|---|---|---|---|---|---|---|---|
| System | A.D.A. Grades K–12 | A.D.A. Grades 7–9 | Population 1930 | System | A.D.A. Grades K–12 | A.D.A. Grades 7–9 | Population 1930 |
| Springfield, Mass. | 24,571 | 5,771 | 149,900 | Hartford, Conn. | 26,215 | 6,282 | 164,072 |
| Trenton, N. J. | 17,836 | 4,368 | 123,356 | Paterson, N. J. | 22,605 | 5,228 | 138,513 |
| Mount Vernon, N. Y. | 9,632 | 2,100 | 61,499 | Passaic, N. J. | 11,435 | 2,726 | 62,959 |
| Pittsfield, Mass. | 8,657 | 1,962 | 49,677 | Perth Amboy, N. J. | 7,595 | 1,987 | 43,516 |
| White Plains, N. Y. | 6,171 | 1,590 | 35,830 | Brookline, Mass. | 5,535 | 1,374 | 47,490 |
| New Brunswick, N. J. | 5,918 | 1,449 | 34,555 | Orange, N. J. | 5,975 | 1,306 | 35,399 |
| West Orange, N. J. | 4,111 | 949 | 24,327 | Hackensack, N. J. | 4,657 | 920 | 24,568 |
| West Springfield, Mass. | 3,369 | 788 | 16,684 | Braintree, Mass. | 3,323 | 728 | 15,712 |
| Northampton, Mass. | 3,344 | 814 | 24,381 | Gardner, Mass. | 2,600 | 763 | 19,399 |
| Long Branch, N. J. | 3,136 | 756 | 18,399 | Englewood, N. J. | 2,952 | 718 | 17,805 |
| Norwood, Mass. | 2,995 | 943 | 15,049 | Milford, Mass. | 2,708 | 645 | 14,741 |
| Adams, Mass. | 1,887 | 516 | 12,697 | Clinton, Mass. | 1,725 | 458 | 12,817 |
| TOTAL | 91,627 | 22,006 | 566,354 | TOTAL | 97,325 | 23,135 | 596,991 |

table each 8–4 system is placed opposite the 6–3–3 system which determined the choice of the former.

The actual costs per pupil in average daily attendance in grades K to 6, 7 to 9, 10 to 12, and K to 12 for the twenty-four selected 6–3–3 and 8–4 systems are presented in Table 25. This table shows that for the two groups the actual per pupil costs vary little. The mean per pupil costs in grades K to 6 in the 6–3–3 systems are $108.35 and in the 8–4 systems, $106.28. Similarly the mean per pupil costs in grades 7 to 9 for the two groups are $135.55 and $132.35; in grades 10 to 12, $174.81 and $173.88; in grades K to 12, $125.53 and $121.78. Hence, while the per pupil costs in the 6–3–3 systems are higher, they are only slightly higher; moreover, they are consistently higher, that is, they are higher for all groups of grades.

The range of per pupil costs in grades 7 to 9 in the 6–3–3 group is from $80.37 to $232.92. The costs in the remaining ten systems tend toward an even distribution between the two extremes as is indicated by a comparison of the median, $131.85, with the mean, $135.55. In the 8–4 group the range for grades 7 to 9 is from $78.47 to $186.71. The remaining systems in the 8–4 group are not so evenly distributed between these two extremes, there being a tendency for a number of the systems to concentrate toward the lower extreme. This is indicated by the fact that the median is $141.12, while the mean is only $132.35. An examination of the per pupil costs in grades K to 6, 10 to 12, and K to 12 for both groups discloses a considerable range with a fairly even distribution within the ranges in every instance. On the whole, then, the twelve systems in each type of organization show a wide range of per pupil costs, but an even distribution of costs within this range for all units of grades.

For the purpose of showing relative costs in the twelve 6–3–3 and the twelve 8–4 systems, Table 26 is presented. In this table costs are reported, not in terms of actual expenditures as is done in Table 25, but in terms of relationship. That is, the costs in grades K to 6 for each system are given an index value of 100, and the costs in the other grade groups are given a proportionate value. On this basis, in White Plains, New York, when per pupil costs in grades K to 6 are given a value of 100, per pupil costs in grades 7 to 9 are 152.9; in grades 10 to 12, 173.9; in grades K to 12, 126.1. These values show relative costs at a glance. For example, they

TABLE 25

COSTS PER PUPIL IN AVERAGE DAILY ATTENDANCE IN GRADES K TO 6, 7 TO 9, 10 TO 12, AND K TO 12 FOR TWELVE SELECTED 6-3-3 SYSTEMS AND TWELVE SELECTED 8-4 SYSTEMS

| System | 6-3-3 Systems | | | | System | 8-4 Systems | | | |
|---|---|---|---|---|---|---|---|---|---|
| | Grades K-6 | Grades 7-9 | Grades 10-12 | Grades K-12 | | Grades K-6 | Grades 7-9 | Grades 10-12 | Grades K-12 |
| Springfield, Mass. | $102.89 | $140.20 | $194.31 | $127.09 | Hartford, Conn. | $120.79 | $163.79 | $208.63 | $143.35 |
| Trenton, N. J. | 114.25 | 157.11 | 178.07 | 132.65 | Paterson, N. J. | 121.60 | 151.57 | 188.71 | 136.93 |
| Mount Vernon, N. Y. | 160.44 | 194.39 | 225.44 | 178.93 | Passaic, N. J. | 109.39 | 145.09 | 175.24 | 123.81 |
| Pittsfield, Mass. | 85.13 | 95.97 | 113.03 | 91.44 | Perth Amboy, N. J. | 99.82 | 116.98 | 145.51 | 108.89 |
| White Plains, N. Y. | 152.29 | 232.92 | 264.91 | 192.11 | Brookline, Mass. | 136.35 | 182.40 | 208.70 | 161.48 |
| New Brunswick, N. J. | 104.72 | 191.41 | 161.58 | 121.11 | Orange, N. J. | 102.03 | 137.15 | 161.48 | 115.69 |
| West Orange, N. J. | 118.03 | 158.37 | 196.51 | 139.25 | Hackensack, N. J. | 141.60 | 186.71 | 191.32 | 158.41 |
| West Springfield, Mass. | 91.65 | 112.87 | 144.41 | 103.98 | Braintree, Mass. | 77.48 | 97.16 | 181.93 | 95.90 |
| Northampton, Mass. | 81.04 | 92.71 | 122.67 | 91.07 | Gardner, Mass. | 72.19 | 81.36 | 121.65 | 85.17 |
| Long Branch, N. J. | 115.48 | 133.28 | 200.14 | 132.78 | Englewood, N. J. | 142.13 | 166.70 | 266.12 | 164.28 |
| Norwood, Mass. | 100.45 | 96.96 | 191.66 | 116.04 | Milford, Mass. | 67.94 | 78.47 | 110.19 | 76.02 |
| Adams, Mass. | 73.89 | 80.37 | 105.00 | 79.93 | Clinton, Mass. | 84.02 | 80.86 | 127.07 | 91.47 |
| MEAN | $108.35 | $135.55 | $174.81 | $125.53 | MEAN | $106.28 | $132.35 | $173.88 | $121.78 |
| MEDIAN | 103.80 | 131.85 | 184.86 | 124.10 | MEDIAN | 105.71 | 141.12 | 178.58 | 119.75 |

TABLE 26

RELATIVE COSTS PER PUPIL IN AVERAGE DAILY ATTENDANCE IN GRADES K TO 6, 7 TO 9, 10 TO 12, AND K TO 12 FOR TWELVE SELECTED 6-3-3 SYSTEMS AND TWELVE SELECTED 8-4 SYSTEMS

### 6-3-3 Systems

| System | Ratio of per Pupil Costs When Costs in Grades K-6 Equal 100 | | | |
|---|---|---|---|---|
| | Grades K-6 | Grades 7-9 | Grades 10-12 | Grades K-12 |
| White Plains, N. Y. | 100 | 152.9 | 173.9 | 126.1 |
| Trenton, N. J. | 100 | 187.5 | 155.9 | 116.1 |
| Springfield, Mass. | 100 | 136.3 | 188.8 | 123.5 |
| West Orange, N. J. | 100 | 134.2 | 166.5 | 118.0 |
| New Brunswick, N. J. | 100 | 125.5 | 154.3 | 115.6 |
| West Springfield, Mass. | 100 | 123.1 | 157.6 | 113.4 |
| Mount Vernon, N. Y. | 100 | 121.2 | 140.5 | 111.5 |
| Long Branch, N. J. | 100 | 115.4 | 173.3 | 115.0 |
| Northampton, Mass. | 100 | 114.4 | 151.4 | 112.4 |
| Pittsfield, Mass. | 100 | 112.7 | 132.8 | 107.4 |
| Adams, Mass. | 100 | 108.8 | 142.1 | 108.2 |
| Norwood, Mass. | 100 | 96.5 | 190.8 | 115.5 |
| MEAN | 100 | 125.1 | 161.3 | 115.9 |
| MEDIAN | 100 | 122.2 | 156.7 | 115.2 |

### 8-4 Systems

| System | Ratio of per Pupil Costs When Costs in Grades K-6 Equal 100 | | | |
|---|---|---|---|---|
| | Grades K-6 | Grades 7-9 | Grades 10-12 | Grades K-12 |
| Hartford, Conn. | 100 | 135.6 | 172.7 | 118.7 |
| Orange, N. J. | 100 | 134.4 | 158.3 | 113.4 |
| Brookline, Mass. | 100 | 133.8 | 153.1 | 118.3 |
| Passaic, N. J. | 100 | 132.6 | 160.2 | 113.2 |
| Hackensack, N. J. | 100 | 131.9 | 135.1 | 111.9 |
| Braintree, Mass. | 100 | 125.4 | 234.8 | 123.8 |
| Paterson, N. J. | 100 | 124.6 | 155.2 | 112.6 |
| Englewood, N. J. | 100 | 117.3 | 187.2 | 115.6 |
| Perth Amboy, N. J. | 100 | 117.2 | 145.8 | 109.1 |
| Milford, Mass. | 100 | 115.5 | 162.2 | 111.9 |
| Gardner, Mass. | 100 | 112.7 | 168.5 | 118.0 |
| Clinton, Mass. | 100 | 96.2 | 151.2 | 108.9 |
| MEAN | 100 | 124.5 | 163.6 | 114.6 |
| MEDIAN | 100 | 125.0 | 159.2 | 113.3 |

show that the highest relative per pupil costs in grades 7 to 9 in the 6–3–3 group are in White Plains, where they are 52.9 per cent above the per pupil costs in grades K to 6, and the lowest relative costs are in Norwood, Massachusetts, where grades 7 to 9 have a value of only 96.5 when costs in grades K to 6 are 100, or 3.5 per cent less than in grades K to 6. Likewise, this table shows that in the 8–4 group the highest relative per pupil costs in grades 7 to 9 are in Hartford, Connecticut, where they are 35.6 per cent higher than in grades K to 6; and the lowest relative per pupil costs in grades 7 to 9 are in Clinton, Massachusetts, where they are 3.8 per cent less than in grades K to 6.

While the mean is perhaps a better measure of central tendency in the two groups of systems reported here,[3] both the mean and the median are given in Table 26. When the mean per pupil costs in grades K to 6 are given a value of 100, the mean relative per pupil costs in grades 7 to 9 in the 6–3–3 systems are 125.1 and in the 8–4 systems are 124.5. In other words, the per pupil costs in grades 7 to 9 vary from those in grades K to 6 in both types of organization to almost identically the same degree, being only .6 per cent higher in the 6–3–3 systems than in the 8–4. The slightness of this difference might be anticipated from Table 25 where it will be seen that the means of the *actual* costs in the various grade groups are similar in amount in the two types of organization.

When the median is used as a measure of central tendency, the per pupil costs in grades 7 to 9 in the 6–3–3 group are found to be 22.2 per cent above those in grades K to 6, and in the 8–4 systems, 25 per cent above. This would indicate relative per pupil costs in grades 7 to 9 2.8 per cent higher in the 8–4 systems than in the 6–3–3 systems. However, as has been indicated, probably less reliance should be placed upon the median than upon the mean.

It appears, then, from Tables 25 and 26 that in actual amounts and in terms of relative amounts the per pupil costs in grades 7 to 9 are substantially the same in the junior high school group as they are in the non-junior high school group. This finding, which is contrary to a considerable body of common opinion, challenges the assumption that per pupil costs in grades 7 to 9 which are higher than per pupil costs in grades K to 6 in 6–3–3 systems prove that

[3]See H. E. Garrett, *Statistics in Psychology and Education*, p. 50, Longmans, Green and Company, 1926. The mean should be used when the highest reliability is sought, when each score or measure should have equal weight in determining the central tendency, and when there are no extreme measures which would affect the mean disproportionately.

costs in grades 7 to 9 in 6–3–3 systems are higher than in these same grades in 8–4 systems.[4]   Therefore, the question should be raised as to whether or not the results found here show that the per pupil costs in grades 7 to 9 in 6–3–3 systems are lower, or that the per pupil costs in grades 7 to 9 in 8–4 systems are higher, than might have been expected.   If the mean of the relative per pupil costs in grades 7 to 9 in the twelve selected 6–3–3 systems is compared with the mean in the one hundred seven 6–3–3 systems (see Table 2), it will be seen that the former is somewhat lower than the latter, 125.1 compared with 133.8.   This would seem to indicate that part of the answer lies in the fact that the twelve selected 6–3–3 systems are somewhat below the average for all the 6–3–3 systems in six eastern states in per pupil costs.   This, however, might have been anticipated, since the twelve systems were selected from Massachusetts, New Jersey, and New York where junior high school costs are relatively low, and no systems were selected from Connecticut, Pennsylvania, and Rhode Island where junior high school costs are relatively high.   They were so chosen, not because of a deliberate choice of states where relative costs are low, but because they best fulfilled the requirements set up in this study and because they were most accessible.   At the time they were selected no cost data were available for the one hundred seven 6–3–3 systems.[5]

Although the twelve selected 6–3–3 systems show relative costs in grades 7 to 9 which are somewhat lower than in the 107 systems, it is to costs in grades 7 to 9 in the 8–4 systems that one must look for the major explanation of similar relative costs in the two selected groups of opposed organizations.   Here it is that costs are much higher than might have been expected, since it has so often been assumed that costs in grades K to 6 are approximately equal to costs in grades 7 and 8 in 8–4 systems.   This raises still

[4]See Tables 1 and 2 showing higher costs in grades 7 to 9 than in grades K to 6 in 107 6–3–3 systems One of the purposes of the first phase of this study was to secure ample additional data as to variation of costs between grades K to 6 and grades 7 to 9 in 6–3–3 systems to test the assumption that higher costs in grades 7 to 9 than in grades K to 6 in junior high school systems could be taken as evidence of higher relative costs in grades 7 to 9 in reorganized schools than in these same grades in traditional schools.   Tables 1 and 2 show that with very few exceptions costs are higher in grades 7 to 9 than in grades K to 6 in 6–3–3 systems.   Yet Tables 25 and 26 show costs in grades 7 to 9 to be substantially higher than costs in grades K to 6 in 8–4 systems.   See also Tables 27 and 28 showing higher costs in grades 7 and 8 than in grades K to 6 in 8–4 systems.

[5]Perhaps the basic explanation of lower costs in the twelve selected systems is not that they offer fewer standard junior high school features than the average of the 107 systems, because they probably offer more, but that on the whole they are older as reorganized systems.   There is little question but that in some states, at least, the systems which have been reorganized the longest tend to show the least variation in costs between grades 7 to 9 and K to 6.

another issue, the degree to which grades 7 and 8 and grade 9 as separate units determine the consistently higher per pupil costs in grades 7 to 9 than in grades K to 6 in the twelve selected 8–4 systems.

The actual and relative per pupil costs in grades 7 and 8 and in grade 9 in the twelve 8–4 organizations are given in Tables 27 and 28. These tables indicate a number of things. In every system the per pupil costs in grades 7 and 8 are higher than in grades K to 6, ranging from less than 1 per cent to 38 per cent, with mean per pupil costs for the twelve systems 21.6 per cent higher in grades 7 and 8 than in grades K to 6. In every system except one the per pupil costs are higher in grade 9 than in grades K to 6; in most instances they are substantially higher so that the mean per pupil costs in grade 9 are 31 per cent higher than the mean per pupil costs in grades K to 6. Thus it will be seen that grade 9 in the twelve systems shows a somewhat higher relative per pupil cost than grades 7 and 8, 131.0 compared with 121.6.

Tables 27 and 28 disclose other facts. They show that although the mean per pupil costs in grade 9 are somewhat higher than in grades 7 to 9, in six systems the per pupil costs in grade 9 are less than in grades 7 and 8. They also show that in every system ex-

TABLE 27

COSTS PER PUPIL IN AVERAGE DAILY ATTENDANCE IN GRADES K TO 6, 7 AND 8, 9, 7 TO 9, AND 10 TO 12 FOR TWELVE SELECTED 8–4 SYSTEMS

| SYSTEM | COST PER PUPIL | | | | |
|---|---|---|---|---|---|
| | Grades K–6 | Grades 7–8 | Grade 9 | Grades 7–9 | Grades 10–12 |
| Hartford, Conn. | $120.79 | $153.94 | $186.83 | $163.79 | $208.63 |
| Paterson, N. J. | 121.60 | 151.80 | 151.09 | 151.57 | 188.71 |
| Passaic, N. J. | 109.39 | 150.00 | 135.66 | 145.09 | 175.24 |
| Perth Amboy, N. J. | 99.82 | 121.72 | 106.29 | 116.98 | 145.51 |
| Brookline, Mass. | 136.35 | 186.82 | 173.29 | 182.40 | 208.70 |
| Orange, N. J. | 102.03 | 138.36 | 134.63 | 137.15 | 161.48 |
| Hackensack, N. J. | 141.60 | 172.00 | 214.68 | 186.71 | 191.32 |
| Braintree, Mass. | 77.48 | 87.26 | 118.06 | 97.16 | 181.93 |
| Gardner, Mass. | 72.19 | 76.21 | 91.04 | 81.36 | 121.65 |
| Englewood, N. J. | 142.13 | 157.14 | 181.30 | 166.70 | 266.12 |
| Milford, Mass. | 67.94 | 71.47 | 99.87 | 78.48 | 110.19 |
| Clinton, Mass. | 84.02 | 84.06 | 77.51 | 80.86 | 127.07 |
| MEAN | $106.28 | $129.23 | $139.19 | $132.35 | $173.88 |
| MEDIAN | 105.71 | 144.18 | 135.14 | 141.12 | 178.58 |

TABLE 28

RELATIVE COSTS PER PUPIL IN AVERAGE DAILY ATTENDANCE IN GRADES K
TO 6, 7 AND 8, 9, 7 TO 9, AND 10 TO 12 FOR TWELVE SELECTED 8–4 SYSTEMS

| SYSTEM | RATIO OF PER PUPIL COSTS WHEN COSTS IN GRADES K–6 EQUAL 100 | | | | |
| --- | --- | --- | --- | --- | --- |
| | Grades K–6 | Grades 7–8 | Grade 9 | Grades 7–9 | Grades 10–12 |
| Hartford, Conn. | 100 | 127.4 | 154.7 | 135.6 | 172.7 |
| Paterson, N. J. | 100 | 124.8 | 124.2 | 124.6 | 155.2 |
| Passaic, N. J. | 100 | 137.1 | 124.0 | 132.6 | 160.2 |
| Perth Amboy, N. J. | 100 | 121.9 | 106.5 | 117.2 | 145.8 |
| Brookline, Mass. | 100 | 138.0 | 127.1 | 133.8 | 153.1 |
| Orange, N. J. | 100 | 135.6 | 131.9 | 134.4 | 158.3 |
| Hackensack, N. J. | 100 | 121.5 | 151.6 | 131.9 | 135.1 |
| Braintree, Mass. | 100 | 112.6 | 152.4 | 125.4 | 234.8 |
| Gardner, Mass. | 100 | 105.6 | 126.1 | 112.7 | 168.5 |
| Englewood, N. J. | 100 | 110.6 | 127.6 | 117.3 | 187.2 |
| Milford, Mass. | 100 | 105.2 | 147.0 | 115.5 | 162.2 |
| Clinton, Mass. | 100 | 100.0 | 92.2 | 96.2 | 151.2 |
| MEAN | 100 | 121.6 | 131.0 | 124.5 | 163.6 |
| MEDIAN | 100 | 121.7 | 127.3 | 125.0 | 159.2 |

cept one, that of Hackensack, New Jersey, the per pupil costs in
grade 9 are less than in grades 10 to 12. Moreover, in grades 10 to
12 the mean per pupil costs are 63.6 per cent higher than in grades
K to 6, whereas in grade 9 they are only 31 per cent higher, that is,
the excess of costs in grades 10 to 12 over costs in grades K to 6 is
more than double the excess of costs in grade 9 over costs in grades
K to 6. These facts indicate that for these twelve 8–4 systems it
would be a serious error to assume that the per pupil costs in grades
7 and 8 are the same as the per pupil costs in grades K to 8, or that
the per pupil costs in grade 9 are the same as in grades 9 to 12.
Yet these have been rather common assumptions in the past.

Because the above results are somewhat contrary to expectation
and not in harmony with what were believed to be valid assumptions, it should be indicated at this point that much caution was
exercised and considerable labor expended to check and recheck
the data here offered. While some superintendents of schools or
directors of research were willing to concede the possibility of
somewhat higher costs in grades 7 and 8 than in grades K to 6,
few were prepared for the amount of variation usually found, and
none was prepared for the situations which showed higher costs in

grades 7 and 8 than in grade 9. In almost every case such interest in these results was shown by school officials that they had the data rechecked.

In no case, except one, were there discovered any unusual conditions which might have been reflected in per pupil costs. In 1930–1931 in Perth Amboy, New Jersey, an attempt was being made to discard a system of mid-year promotions. As a result of this action a large number of pupils from grade 8A were passed into grade 9 at the beginning of the year, but the instructional staff of grade 9 was increased only slightly. This meant an abnormally large pupil-teacher ratio in grade 9 which would tend to lower per pupil costs in that grade. Grade 9 had not been relieved of any pupils by passing 9A pupils to grade 10. On the other hand, grades 7 and 8 were not materially affected because to a considerable extent grade 7A was passed into grade 8, and grade 6A into grade 7, thus maintaining approximately normal numbers in those grades. This condition probably accounts in part for the fact that in Perth Amboy, although per pupil costs in grades 7 and 8 are 21.9 per cent higher than in grades K to 6, in grade 9 they are only 6.5 per cent higher than in grades K to 6.

Hackensack, New Jersey, alone shows higher costs in grade 9 than in grades 10 to 12. This fact appears to set the system aside as an unusual case since not only do all the other systems show a reversal of this situation but they show substantially higher costs in grades 10 to 12 than in grade 9 (see Table 28). Apparently the situation in Hackensack is due primarily to the fact that class-size in grade 9 is approximately equal to that in other grades and the teachers who spend the major portion of their time in grade 9 are on the whole those with the highest salaries. In the other systems it was found that there was a tendency for classes in grade 9 to average considerably larger than classes in grades 10 to 12, and for teachers with the higher salaries to spend proportionately more of their time in grades 10, 11, and 12 than in grade 9.

The discussion of data up to this point has been largely in terms of the averages or arithmetic means of the two selected groups of systems. The use of this mean, however, gives equal value to each of the systems in the group. Since it was obtained by adding the actual or relative per pupil costs in the various systems of each group and then dividing this sum by twelve, it is apparent that the larger systems have no greater influence in this measure of central tendency than the smaller ones. When, on the other hand, the total costs of the twelve systems in each group, instead of per pupil costs, are added, and this sum divided by the total average daily attendance in each group, the resulting figure is one which gives weight to the various systems in each group in proportion to the total costs and the total average daily attendance. When this is done for the twelve systems in each type of organization the results are as given in Table 29. In both the 6–3–3 systems and the 8–4 systems the costs are materially increased for every grade group.

TABLE 29

COSTS PER PUPIL IN AVERAGE DAILY ATTENDANCE IN GRADES K TO 6, 7 TO 9, 10 TO 12, AND K TO 12 FOR TWELVE SELECTED 6–3–3 SYSTEMS AND TWELVE SELECTED 8–4 SYSTEMS, BY TYPE OF ORGANIZATION

*Pupils as Units*

| TYPE OF ORGANIZATION | COST PER PUPIL | | | |
|---|---|---|---|---|
| | Grades K–6 | Grades 7–9 | Grades 10–12 | Grades K–12 |
| 6–3–3 | $112.11 | $145.46 | $185.43 | $131.51 |
| 8–4 | 114.54 | 146.60 | 186.68 | 131.59 |

This results from the fact that on the whole the larger systems in each group have a somewhat higher per pupil cost than the smaller systems. If Table 29 is compared with Table 25 it will be noted that when pupils are taken as the unit in obtaining a measure of central tendency, the per pupil costs in all groups of grades in the 6–3–3 systems are below those in the 8–4 systems, whereas when the individual systems are used as the unit in obtaining a measure of central tendency (the mean) the per pupil costs in each grade group in the 6–3–3 systems are higher than in the corresponding grade group in the 8–4 systems. This reversal of cost situations obtained by using pupils instead of systems as the unit is not of importance and indicates merely that per pupil costs in the larger 8–4 systems are higher in relation to those in the smaller than are per pupil costs in the larger 6–3–3 systems in relation to those in the smaller.

Relative per pupil costs, with pupils rather than systems as units, are shown in Table 30. In spite of the fact that by this method actual costs were increased more in the 8–4 systems than in the 6–3–3 systems, relative costs in grades 7 to 9 in the 6–3–3 systems show a slight gain over relative costs in grades 7 to 9 in the 8–4. However, the difference is small, 1.7 per cent (129.7–128.0).

When the twelve 6–3–3 systems and the twelve 8–4 systems are considered as a whole there appears to be nothing to indicate that the actual or the relative per pupil costs are significantly higher in one type of organization than in another. Mean actual costs are slightly higher in the 6–3–3 systems than in the 8–4, $135.55 compared with $132.35. The median of actual costs is considerably lower in the 6–3–3 systems than in the 8–4, $131.85 as opposed to $141.12. When pupils instead of systems are used as the unit for

TABLE 30

RELATIVE COSTS PER PUPIL IN AVERAGE DAILY ATTENDANCE IN GRADES K TO 6, 7 TO 9, 10 TO 12, AND K TO 12 FOR TWELVE SELECTED 6–3–3 SYSTEMS AND TWELVE SELECTED 8–4 SYSTEMS, BY TYPE OF ORGANIZATION

*Pupils as Units*

| TYPE OF ORGANIZATION | RATIO OF PER PUPIL COSTS WHEN COSTS IN GRADES K–6 EQUAL 100 | | | |
| --- | --- | --- | --- | --- |
| | Grades K–6 | Grades 7–9 | Grades 10–12 | Grades K–12 |
| 6–3–3 | 100 | 129.7 | 165.4 | 117.3 |
| 8–4 | 100 | 128.0 | 163.0 | 114.9 |

obtaining a measure of central tendency, it is found that again the costs are slightly lower in the 6–3–3 systems than in the 8–4 systems, $145.46 compared with $146.60.

However, it is upon relative rather than upon actual costs that reliance is placed in this investigation, although actual costs are so nearly identical in all groups of grades in both types of organization as to merit some attention. Mean relative per pupil costs in grades 7 to 9 are only slightly higher in the 6–3–3 type of organization than in the 8–4, 125.1 compared with 124.5, whereas the median is somewhat lower in the 6–3–3 type, 122.2 as opposed to 125.0. The weighted average obtained by using pupils as units shows relative per pupil costs to be somewhat higher in the 6–3–3 systems than in the 8–4 systems, 129.7 compared with 128.0.

# VIII

# Analysis of Per Pupil Costs by Character in Grades 7 to 9 in Twelve 6-3-3 and Twelve 8-4 Systems

THE data reported in the previous chapter indicating that there are no appreciable differences between the twelve 6–3–3 and the twelve 8–4 systems in per pupil costs in grades 7 to 9 are for the totals of all items of expense and present no evidence in regard to the origins of these totals. Similarity in totals, however, is no guarantee of similarity in the various items of cost. The purpose of this chapter is to examine in both types of organization how per pupil costs in grades 7 to 9 vary from those in grades K to 6 for each of the items of character classification and to present certain causal evidence relative to the variations found.

Average costs by character in grades K to 6, 7 to 9, 10 to 12, and K to 12 for both types of organization are shown in Table 31. These average costs are not mean costs but are obtained by adding the total costs of the twelve systems for each character item in grades K to 6, 7 to 9, 10 to 12, and K to 12 and dividing by the average daily attendance in these various grade groups. This table shows actual instead of relative costs. However, because the two types of organization show similar per pupil costs in grades K to 6, 7 to 9, 10 to 12, and K to 12 for all items of expense combined (see totals, Table 31), it is possible to see at a glance any unusual cost variations by character between the two groups of systems in any of the grade units without obscuring actual costs by converting them into relative costs.

For instruction salaries, instructional costs other than salaries, and operation, almost identical amounts are spent per pupil in the two types of organization in grades K to 12. In these same grades the 6–3–3 systems spend substantially more per pupil for general control, auxiliary agencies, and fixed charges and substantially less for maintenance and for coördinate activities. This same tendency is shown in grades 7 to 9. In fact, the per pupil cost varia-

TABLE 31

AVERAGE* PER PUPIL COSTS, BY CHARACTER, IN GRADES K TO 6, 7 TO 9, 10 TO 12, AND K TO 12 IN TWELVE SELECTED 6-3-3 SYSTEMS AND TWELVE SELECTED 8-4 SYSTEMS

Pupils as Units

| Grades | Type of Organization | General Control | Instruction Salaries | Instruction Other | Operation | Maintenance | Coördinate Activities | Auxiliary Agencies | Fixed Charges | Totals |
|---|---|---|---|---|---|---|---|---|---|---|
| K-6 | 6-3-3 | $4.64 | $ 78.01 | $ 5.14 | $12.26 | $5.39 | $2.95 | $1.62 | $2.10 | $112.11 |
| K-6 | 8-4 | 3.46 | 79.62 | 5.81 | 12.79 | 7.88 | 3.19 | .95 | .84 | 114.54 |
| 7-9 | 6-3-3 | 5.37 | 104.15 | 8.18 | 14.21 | 5.50 | 2.53 | 3.19 | 2.33 | 145.46 |
| 7-9 | 8-4 | 3.89 | 105.59 | 8.23 | 14.54 | 8.66 | 3.33 | 1.24 | 1.13 | 146.61 |
| 10-12 | 6-3-3 | 5.55 | 132.50 | 13.38 | 20.35 | 5.93 | 1.58 | 2.95 | 3.19 | 185.43 |
| 10-12 | 8-4 | 4.50 | 139.86 | 10.55 | 16.96 | 7.84 | 3.25 | 1.88 | 1.84 | 186.68 |
| K-12 | 6-3-3 | 4.96 | 92.75 | 7.15 | 13.98 | 5.50 | 2.64 | 2.21 | 2.32 | 131.51 |
| K-12 | 8-4 | 3.70 | 93.67 | 7.00 | 13.75 | 8.06 | 3.23 | 1.14 | 1.04 | 131.59 |

*This is the weighted average in which the various systems are given a weight in proportion to total expenditures and total average daily attendance.

tions between the two types of organization are less in grades 7 to 9 than in grades K to 6, and considerably less than in grades 10 to 12 for the major items, instruction and operation. For general control, auxiliary agencies, and fixed charges, all grade groups in the 6–3–3 systems consistently spend more per pupil than in the 8–4 systems. For maintenance and coördinate activities in all grade groups the 6–3–3 systems consistently spend less than the 8–4 systems.

The per pupil costs for the item instruction salaries in both grades K to 6 and 7 to 9 seem surprisingly similar in amount as between the two types of organization, particularly since this item is of considerable size and therefore might easily fluctuate much more than those items which are smaller in amount. It appears from Table 31 that for instruction the two types of organization tend to spend the same amounts, except that in grades 10 to 12 in the 8–4 systems the per pupil costs are somewhat higher for instruction salaries and somewhat lower for instructional costs other than salaries. It also appears from this table that the 6–3–3 systems tend to purchase more of those services which fall within the classification of auxiliary agencies than do the 8–4 systems, but less of those classed as coördinate activities. The latter was noticeable at the time the cost figures were being secured in the field. It was particularly noticeable that whereas medical, dental, and nursing services were purchased to about the same degree in the lower grades in both types of organization (see a per pupil cost of $2.95 in 6–3–3 systems and $3.19 in 8–4 systems in grades K to 6), the 8–4 systems tended to continue or even increase this service in the upper grades (see a per pupil cost of $3.33 in grades 7 to 9 and $3.25 in grades 10 to 12), while the 6–3–3 systems tended to lessen this service in the upper grades, particularly in the senior high school (see a per pupil cost of $2.53 in grades 7 to 9 and $1.58 in grades 10 to 12).

The fact that maintenance costs in the 6–3–3 type of organization are substantially and consistently lower than those in the 8–4 type probably is due not to chance but to the fact that the reorganization from the 8–4 to the 6–3–3 plan was partly determined by and usually accompanied by a building program of considerable importance. This probably means, although no definite check was made to ascertain the exact date or types of construction, that on the whole the buildings of the 6–3–3 systems

are newer and hence require less expenditure for upkeep. It
might be expected from this that operating expenses would be
less in the 6–3–3 systems than in the 8–4, but it will be noted
that the per pupil costs in the 6–3–3 systems are only slightly
less in grades K to 6 and 7 to 9 and that they are actually more
in grades 10 to 12.

The consistently and substantially higher costs for fixed charges
in the 6–3–3 systems apparently are due less to differences in type
of organization than to other circumstances. The largest item
of cost for fixed charges in many systems is that part of the teachers' pension expense which is borne by the local school system.
Practices in this matter vary considerably from state to state and
it is to such practices rather than to variations between types of
organization that the cost differences between the twelve 6–3–3
and the twelve 8–4 systems for fixed charges may be largely
traced.

The above cost comparison by character between types of organization is direct rather than relative. Moreover, it is in terms
of averages for the two types of organization, no data for individual systems being indicated. Tables 32 and 33 show by character the differences in actual per pupil costs between grades 7
to 9 and K to 6 for each system in the 6–3–3 and the 8–4 groups,
respectively. That is, in Springfield, Massachusetts, a 6–3–3
system, per pupil costs are $.73 higher in grades 7 to 9 than in
grades K to 6 for general control, $30.55 higher for instruction
salaries, $2.32 higher for instructional costs other than salaries,
$3.93 higher for operation, $.41 higher for auxiliary agencies, and
$.04 higher for fixed charges; whereas per pupil costs are $.20
lower for maintenance and $.47 lower for coördinate activities,
making a total of $37.31 higher per pupil costs in grades 7 to 9
than in grades K to 6. In Hartford, Connecticut, an 8–4 system,
grades 7 to 9 show higher per pupil costs than grades K to 6 for
every item, ranging from $.24 higher for fixed charges to $31.61
higher for instructional salaries, with a total of $43.00 higher per
pupil costs in grades 7 to 9 than in grades K to 6.

When the mean is used as a measure of central tendency, per
pupil cost differences in the 6–3–3 group range from $.12 less to
$21.21 more in grades 7 to 9 than in K to 6, with two items, main-
tenance and coördinate activities, showing lower costs in grades
7 to 9. In the 8–4 systems the mean shows only one item, co-

TABLE 32

AMOUNTS THAT PER PUPIL COSTS IN GRADES 7 TO 9 EXCEED PER PUPIL COSTS IN GRADES K TO 6 FOR TWELVE SELECTED 6-3-3 SYSTEMS, BY CHARACTER

| System | General Control | Instruction Salaries | Instruction Other | Operation | Maintenance | Coördinate Activities | Auxiliary Agencies | Fixed Charges | Totals |
|---|---|---|---|---|---|---|---|---|---|
| Springfield, Mass. | $ .73 | $30.55 | $2.32 | $3.93 | $—.20* | $—.47 | $ .41 | $ .04 | $87.31 |
| Trenton, N. J. | 1.11 | 29.50 | 5.46 | 2.85 | 1.13 | .00 | 3.37 | —.56 | 42.86 |
| Mount Vernon, N. Y. | 1.08 | 28.42 | 2.71 | 2.05 | —.43 | —1.10 | —.43 | 1.65 | 33.95 |
| Pittsfield, Mass. | .31 | 13.04 | .41 | —1.85 | —.67 | .26 | —1.01 | .35 | 10.84 |
| White Plains, N. Y. | 1.62 | 62.16 | 6.36 | 1.05 | 1.39 | —.56 | 6.23 | 2.48 | 80.63 |
| New Brunswick, N. J. | .41 | 22.96 | 1.90 | —.95 | .91 | .00 | 1.46 | .00 | 26.69 |
| West Orange, N. J. | 1.39 | 26.49 | 5.30 | 5.38 | —.86 | —.63 | 3.87 | —.60 | 40.34 |
| West Springfield, Mass. | .02 | 6.41 | 4.96 | 3.37 | 1.08 | —.74 | 5.91 | .21 | 21.22 |
| Northampton, Mass. | —.21 | 11.15 | 2.49 | —.87 | .25 | —1.33 | .13 | .06 | 11.67 |
| Long Branch, N. J. | .57 | 28.24 | —1.59 | —5.65 | —2.11 | —1.12 | —.38 | —.16 | 17.80 |
| Norwood, Mass. | —.66 | —6.69 | .30 | 2.43 | 1.57 | —.57 | —.27 | .40 | —3.49 |
| Adams, Mass. | .08 | 2.27 | 1.84 | 3.11 | —3.51 | —.83 | 3.38 | .41 | 6.48 |
| Mean | $ .54 | $21.21 | $2.70 | $1.23 | $—.12 | $—.59 | $1.89 | $ .33 | $27.19 |

*Minus indicates higher per pupil costs in grades K to 6 than in grades 7 to 9.

TABLE 33

AMOUNTS THAT PER PUPIL COSTS IN GRADES 7 TO 9 EXCEED PER PUPIL COSTS IN GRADES K TO 6 FOR TWELVE SELECTED 8-4 SYSTEMS, BY CHARACTER

| System | General Control | Instruction Salaries | Instruction Other | Operation | Maintenance | Coördinate Activities | Auxiliary Agencies | Fixed Charges | Totals |
|---|---|---|---|---|---|---|---|---|---|
| Hartford, Conn. | $ .51 | $31.61 | $2.68 | $4.55 | $1.29 | $1.51 | $ .61 | $ .24 | $43.00 |
| Paterson, N. J. | .26 | 29.98 | 1.31 | —.89* | —.37 | —.46 | —.50 | .64 | 29.97 |
| Passaic, N. J. | .85 | 31.82 | 1.05 | 1.77 | .28 | —.25 | —.11 | .29 | 35.70 |
| Perth Amboy, N. J. | .40 | 13.65 | 3.90 | —.61 | —.11 | —.03 | .03 | —.08 | 17.15 |
| Orange, N. J. | .03 | 22.43 | 6.03 | 3.74 | 3.01 | —.92 | .80 | .00 | 35.12 |
| Brookline, Mass. | .98 | 34.53 | 1.70 | 5.31 | 2.77 | —.75 | 1.21 | .30 | 46.05 |
| Hackensack, N. J. | 1.02 | 39.72 | 5.30 | —1.35 | .67 | —.20 | —.04 | .00 | 45.12 |
| Braintree, Mass. | .22 | 12.10 | 2.02 | 1.20 | —.07 | .04 | 3.67 | .50 | 19.68 |
| Englewood, N. J. | .24 | 12.02 | 3.87 | 2.47 | 5.93 | .08 | —.39 | .35 | 24.57 |
| Milford, Mass. | .21 | 7.96 | 1.73 | —.06 | —.13 | .39 | .37 | .06 | 10.53 |
| Gardner, Mass. | .15 | 6.65 | 2.46 | .86 | —.16 | —.68 | —.31 | .20 | 9.17 |
| Clinton, Mass. | —.40 | —2.13 | 1.34 | —1.31 | —.53 | —.49 | .26 | .10 | —3.16 |
| Mean | $ .37 | $20.03 | $2.78 | $ 1.31 | $1.05 | $—.15 | $ .47 | $ .22 | $26.08 |

*Minus indicates higher per pupil costs in grades K to 6 than in grades 7 to 9.

ordinate activities, costing less in grades 7 to 9 than in grades K to 6. It should be noted at this point that the means for the various items in Tables 32 and 33 were not derived from Table 31. For example, if the per pupil costs for instruction salaries in grades K to 6 in the 6–3–3 systems, as given in Table 31 ($78.01), are subtracted from the per pupil costs for instruction salaries in grades 7 to 9 ($104.15), the difference is $26.14 and not $21.21 as given for the mean of the differences in instructional salaries in the twelve 6–3–3 systems (Table 32). This apparent discrepancy is because the figures in Table 31 are based on a weighted average, as has been explained, whereas the means given in Tables 32 and 33 are not weighted but give equal value to each of the twelve systems. Table 31 might have been given in terms of the arithmetic mean, in which case the means in Tables 32 and 33 could have been derived directly from Table 31. However, it was thought best to forego consistency in the tables for the purpose of showing averages obtained by the two different methods. In order to determine differences in results by the two methods of obtaining measures of central tendency, it is necessary only to subtract per pupil costs in grades K to 6 from those in grades 7 to 9 for the various character items in the twelve 6–3–3 and twelve 8–4 systems as given in Table 31 and to compare these differences with the means shown for the various items in Tables 32 and 33.

When the means in Tables 32 and 33 are compared it will be noted that for the items instruction salaries, instruction other than salaries, and operation, the differences in per pupil costs between grades 7 to 9 and K to 6 are similar for the two types of organization. In the twelve 6–3–3 systems per pupil costs in grades 7 to 9 exceed per pupil costs in grades K to 6 $21.21 for instruction salaries, $2.70 for instructional costs other than salaries, and $1.23 for operation; in the 8–4 systems the excesses for these same items are $20.03, $2.78, and $1.31, respectively. For maintenance the 6–3–3 systems show a lower cost in grades 7 to 9 than in grades K to 6, while the reverse is true of the 8–4 systems. This is probably because at the time of reorganization the junior high school pupils are usually housed in the new or reconditioned buildings while the elementary pupils remain in the older buildings so that the latter on the whole would require a greater expenditure for maintenance. In both types of organization the per pupil costs for coördinate activities are less in grades 7 to 9 than in K to 6, although the falling off in costs is relatively much greater in the 6–3–3 systems than in the 8–4. Per pupil costs for auxiliary agencies are higher in grades 7 to 9 than in grades K to 6 in both the 6–3–3 and 8–4 systems, but are considerably higher relatively in the former than in the latter. Both general control and fixed charges show higher costs in the upper grades than in the lower although relatively they are higher in the 6–3–3 organizations than in the 8–4.

When not the means but individual character items are considered, it is found that in one item only, instruction other than salaries in the 8–4 systems, are costs for all twelve systems higher in grades 7 to 9 than in K to 6. For instruction salaries one system in each group of organizations carries higher per pupil costs in the lower grades than in grades 7 to 9. For coördinate activities in the 6–3–3 systems there is only one system showing higher per pupil costs in grades 7 to 9 than in grades K to 6 while there are four such systems in the 8–4 group.

It is not then mere chance which determines that in the twenty-four systems under consideration the means of the differences between grades 7 to 9 and K to 6 for all items (totals) should be almost equal, $27.19 in the 6–3–3 and $26.08 in the 8–4 systems. That is, it is largely a question of corresponding rather than of unlike items balancing each other, hence there appears to be a considerable consistency of costs between the two types of organization, particularly in the items carrying the higher costs. The differences between grades 7 to 9 and K to 6 for the three largest items, instruction salaries, instruction other than salaries, and operation, are very similar in amount. Likewise, costs for general control and fixed charges do not differ greatly in actual amounts, although they would on a percentage basis. The differences are greatest for maintenance and auxiliary agencies; however, because these sums are small and because they tend to balance each other they have little effect on the totals.

It is, however, in Tables 34 and 35 that the relative importance of the various items in determining the total difference may be most readily seen. For example, in the 6–3–3 systems instruction salaries constitute 78 per cent of the total difference between grades 7 to 9 and K to 6 whereas the next highest item, instructional costs other than salaries, is only 9.9 per cent. Likewise, in

TABLE 34

PER CENT THAT EACH CHARACTER ITEM CONTRIBUTES TO TOTAL EXCESS OF COSTS IN GRADES 7 TO 9 OVER K TO 6, FOR TWELVE SELECTED 6-3-3 SYSTEMS

| System | General Control | Instruction Salaries | Instruction Other | Operation | Maintenance | Coördinate Activities | Auxiliary Agencies | Fixed Charges | Totals |
|---|---|---|---|---|---|---|---|---|---|
| | | | | | Item | | | | |
| Springfield, Mass. | 2.0 | 81.9 | 6.2 | 10.5 | — .5* | —1.3 | 1.1 | .1 | 100.0 |
| Trenton, N. J. | 2.6 | 68.8 | 12.7 | 6.7 | 2.6 | .0 | 7.9 | —1.3 | 100.0 |
| Mount Vernon, N. Y. | 3.2 | 83.7 | 8.0 | 6.0 | —1.3 | —3.2 | —1.3 | 4.9 | 100.0 |
| Pittsfield, Mass. | 2.9 | 120.3 | 3.8 | —17.1 | —6.2 | 2.4 | —9.3 | 3.2 | 100.0 |
| White Plains, N. Y. | 2.0 | 77.1 | 7.9 | 1.3 | 1.7 | —.7 | 7.7 | 3.0 | 100.0 |
| New Brunswick, N. J. | 1.5 | 86.0 | 7.1 | —3.5 | 3.4 | .0 | 5.5 | .0 | 100.0 |
| West Orange, N. J. | 3.4 | 65.7 | 13.1 | 13.3 | —2.1 | —1.5 | 9.6 | —1.5 | 100.0 |
| West Springfield, Mass. | .1 | 30.2 | 23.4 | 15.8 | 5.1 | —3.5 | 27.9 | 1.0 | 100.0 |
| Northampton, Mass. | —1.8 | 95.5 | 21.3 | —7.4 | 2.1 | —11.3 | 1.1 | .5 | 100.0 |
| Long Branch, N. J. | 3.2 | 158.6 | —8.9 | —31.8 | —11.9 | —6.2 | —2.1 | —.9 | 100.0 |
| Norwood, Mass. | —18.9 | —191.7 | 8.7 | 69.6 | 45.0 | —16.3 | —7.8 | 11.4 | —100.0 |
| Adams, Mass. | 1.2 | 35.0 | 28.4 | 48.0 | —54.2 | —12.8 | 52.2 | 2.2 | 100.0 |
| Mean | 2.0 | 78.0 | 9.9 | 4.5 | —.4 | —2.2 | 7.0 | 1.2 | 100.0 |

*Minus indicates higher per pupil costs in grades K to 6 than in grades 7 to 9.

TABLE 35

PER CENT THAT EACH CHARACTER ITEM CONTRIBUTES TO TOTAL EXCESS OF COSTS IN GRADES 7 TO 9 OVER GRADES K TO 6, FOR TWELVE SELECTED 8-4 SYSTEMS

| SYSTEM | ITEM | | | | | | | | |
| --- | --- | --- | --- | --- | --- | --- | --- | --- | --- |
| | General Control | Instruction Salaries | Instruction Other | Operation | Maintenance | Coördinate Activities | Auxiliary Agencies | Fixed Charges | Totals |
| Hartford, Conn. | 1.2 | 73.5 | 6.2 | 10.6 | 3.0 | 3.5 | 1.4 | .6 | 100.0 |
| Paterson, N. J. | .9 | 100.0 | 4.4 | -3.0* | -1.2 | -1.5 | -1.7 | 2.1 | 100.0 |
| Passaic, N. J. | 2.4 | 89.1 | 2.9 | 5.0 | .8 | -.7 | -.3 | .8 | 100.0 |
| Perth Amboy, N. J. | 2.3 | 79.6 | 22.7 | -3.5 | -.6 | -.2 | .2 | -.5 | 100.0 |
| Orange, N. J. | .1 | 63.8 | 17.2 | 10.6 | 8.6 | -2.6 | 2.3 | .0 | 100.0 |
| Brookline, Mass. | 2.1 | 75.0 | 3.7 | 11.5 | 6.0 | -1.6 | 2.6 | .7 | 100.0 |
| Hackensack, N. J. | 2.3 | 88.0 | 11.7 | -3.0 | 1.5 | -.4 | -.1 | .0 | 100.0 |
| Braintree, Mass. | 1.1 | 61.5 | 10.3 | 6.1 | -.3 | .2 | 18.6 | 2.5 | 100.0 |
| Englewood, N. J. | 1.0 | 48.9 | 15.8 | 10.1 | 24.1 | .3 | -1.6 | 1.4 | 100.0 |
| Milford, Mass. | 2.0 | 75.6 | 16.4 | -.6 | -1.2 | 3.7 | 3.5 | .6 | 100.0 |
| Gardner, Mass. | 1.6 | 72.5 | 26.8 | 9.4 | -1.7 | -7.4 | -3.4 | 2.2 | 100.0 |
| Clinton, Mass. | -12.7 | -67.4 | 42.4 | -41.4 | -16.8 | -15.5 | 8.2 | 3.2 | 100.0 |
| MEAN | 1.4 | 76.8 | 10.7 | 5.0 | 4.0 | -.5 | 1.8 | .8 | 100.0 |

*Minus indicates higher per pupil costs in grades K to 6 than in grades 7 to 9.

the 8–4 systems instruction salaries are 76.8 per cent of the total difference and the next highest item is other instructional costs, 10.7 per cent. These two items of instruction in each type of organization constitute almost 90 per cent of the per pupil cost difference between grades 7 to 9 and K to 6. Hence while the other items may not be dismissed as of no importance, it is largely to the items of instruction and principally to instruction salaries that one must look for an explanation of the differences in cost between grades 7 to 9 and K to 6 in both the 6–3–3 and 8–4 types of organization.

Tables 9 and 10 show that instruction salaries and instruction other than salaries in the one hundred seven 6–3–3 systems of the six eastern states constitute percentages of the total difference between grades 7 to 9 and grades K to 6 similar to those in the twelve 6–3–3 and twelve 8–4 systems except that Pennsylvania is noticeably lower. Tables 9 and 10, however, are not directly comparable with the means in Tables 34 and 35 since the former are not means but weighted averages of the various systems in each state.

Because per pupil costs in grades 7 to 9 exceed per pupil costs in grades K to 6 in about the same amounts for the item of instruction in the two types of organization ($21.21 in 6–3–3 and $20.03 in 8–4) and because this item in both types of organization constitutes about the same percentage of the total difference between grades 7 to 9 and K to 6 (78.0 per cent in 6–3–3 and 76.8 per cent in 8–4) the fact is not established that the same reasons determine this similarity of differences for the two types of organization. As was indicated in Chapter V two factors enter into the determination of per pupil costs for instructional salaries, the salaries paid the instructional and supervisory staff and the pupil-staff ratio. These two factors may enter in varying amounts into the determination of per pupil salary costs in the two types of organization.

Table 36 shows the pupil-staff ratios in grades K to 6 and 7 to 9 and the amounts by which those in grades K to 6 exceed those in 7 to 9 in the twelve 6–3–3 and the twelve 8–4 systems. In actual numbers this ratio is slightly lower in both grades K to 6 and 7 to 9 in the 6–3–3 systems than in the corresponding grades in the 8–4 systems, 25.4 compared with 26.7 in grades K to 6 and 23.0 compared with 24.2 in grades 7 to 9. However, in terms of

TABLE 36

PUPIL-STAFF RATIOS IN GRADES K TO 6 AND GRADES 7 TO 9 AND AMOUNTS PUPIL-STAFF RATIO IN GRADES K TO 6 EXCEEDS PUPIL-STAFF RATIO IN GRADES 7 TO 9 IN TWELVE SELECTED 6-3-3 SYSTEMS AND TWELVE SELECTED 8-4 SYSTEMS

### 6-3-3 Systems

| System | Grades K-6 | Grades 7-9 | Amounts K-6 Pupil-Staff Ratio Exceeds 7-9 Pupil-Staff Ratio |
|---|---|---|---|
| Springfield, Mass. | 27.1 | 23.2 | 3.9 |
| Trenton, N. J. | 29.0 | 24.4 | 4.6 |
| Mount Vernon, N. Y. | 24.2 | 20.6 | 3.6 |
| Pittsfield, Mass. | 23.3 | 20.2 | 3.1 |
| White Plains, N. Y. | 25.1 | 20.6 | 4.5 |
| New Brunswick, N. J. | 25.7 | 23.6 | 2.1 |
| West Orange, N. J. | 24.6 | 19.0 | 5.6 |
| Northampton, Mass. | 26.0 | 24.7 | 1.3 |
| West Springfield, Mass. | 26.4 | 25.4 | 1.0 |
| Long Branch, N. J. | 24.6 | 21.4 | 3.2 |
| Norwood, Mass. | 22.1 | 26.9 | —4.8* |
| Adams, Mass. | 26.5 | 25.8 | .7 |
| MEAN | 25.4 | 23.0 | 2.4 |

### 8-4 Systems

| System | Grades K-6 | Grades 7-9 | Amounts K-6 Pupil-Staff Ratio Exceeds 7-9 Pupil-Staff Ratio |
|---|---|---|---|
| Hartford, Conn. | 26.2 | 23.5 | 2.7 |
| Paterson, N. J. | 25.5 | 23.0 | 2.5 |
| Passaic, N. J. | 30.5 | 23.4 | 7.1 |
| Perth Amboy, N. J. | 28.4 | 24.9 | 3.5 |
| Orange, N. J. | 28.9 | 28.7 | .2 |
| Brookline, Mass. | 24.6 | 17.4 | 7.2 |
| Hackensack, N. J. | 21.6 | 18.1 | 3.5 |
| Braintree, Mass. | 25.8 | 23.5 | 2.3 |
| Englewood, N. J. | 22.8 | 21.9 | .9 |
| Milford, Mass. | 29.1 | 26.9 | 2.2 |
| Gardner, Mass. | 29.7 | 27.7 | 2.0 |
| Clinton, Mass. | 27.3 | 30.9 | —3.6 |
| MEAN | 26.7 | 24.2 | 2.5 |

*Minus indicates pupil-staff ratio in grades 7 to 9 exceeds pupil-staff ratio in grades K to 6.

differences between grades K to 6 and grades 7 to 9 the 8–4 systems show a slightly greater spread, a difference of 2.5 pupils per teacher in the 8–4 systems compared with a difference of 2.4 pupils per teacher in the 6–3–3 systems. Although care must be exercised in making general statements about costs in relation to pupil-staff ratio, because it requires only a slight difference in the number of pupils per teacher to produce considerable cost differences, it is apparent that a difference of .1 pupil (2.5–2.4) is not substantial enough to cause any appreciable differences in per pupil costs.

Certain data were introduced in Chapter VI, relative to costs in the 6–3–3 and 8–4 systems in Massachusetts, for the purpose of showing that in 8–4 systems pupil-teacher ratio might be less in grades 7 to 9 than in grades K to 6 due to the natural falling off in enrollment in the upper grades. It appears that the results shown in Table 36 might be interpreted as a substantiation of this argument. But this table also shows that in the 6–3–3 systems the pupil-staff ratio in grades 7 to 9 is less than in grades K to 6. This falling off in enrollment should not, however, affect the situation in the reorganized systems to the same extent that it does in the traditional organizations since usually pupils from more than one elementary school are combined in one junior high school and the identity of all classes or teaching units is lost. But in the junior high school systems there appears to be another explanation for smaller pupil-staff ratio in grades 7 to 9 than in grades K to 6. It involves the introduction of certain subjects which appear to require that there be fewer pupils per teacher. It likewise involves the effect of the addition of certain non-teaching staff members on pupil-staff ratio. These matters are discussed in Chapter IX. It is probable that here is one of the major reasons why costs in grades 7 to 9 in 8–4 systems approach those in 6–3–3 systems. In both types of organization pupil-staff ratio (largely determined by pupil-teacher ratio) is less in grades 7 to 9 than in grades K to 6, although apparently it is less for two different reasons.

Per pupil costs for instructional salaries are determined by an additional factor, the salaries paid. The average salaries paid per teacher for all instructional service including all regular full-time and part-time teachers, substitutes, supervisors, and principals in grades K to 6 and 7 to 9 in the twelve 6–3–3 and the twelve 8–4 systems are as indicated in Table 37. Here as in the case of pupil-

TABLE 37

AVERAGE SALARIES PAID STAFF IN GRADES K TO 6 AND GRADES 7 TO 9 AND AMOUNTS AVERAGE SALARY PAID IN GRADES 7 TO 9 EXCEEDS AVERAGE SALARY PAID IN GRADES K TO 6 IN TWELVE SELECTED 6-3-3 AND TWELVE SELECTED 8-4 SYSTEMS

| 6-3-3 SYSTEMS | | | | 8-4 SYSTEMS | | | |
|---|---|---|---|---|---|---|---|
| System | Grades K-6 | Grades 7-9 | Amounts 7-9 Salary Exceeds K-6 Salary | System | Grades K-6 | Grades 7-9 | Amounts 7-9 Salary Exceeds K-6 Salary |
| Springfield, Mass. | $1,945.94 | $2,370.27 | $424.33 | Hartford, Conn. | $1,962.27 | $2,505.32 | $543.05 |
| Trenton, N. J. | 2,328.09 | 2,677.69 | 349.60 | Paterson, N. J. | 2,285.75 | 2,744.58 | 458.83 |
| Mount Vernon, N. Y. | 2,655.70 | 2,841.11 | 185.41 | Passaic, N. J. | 2,463.44 | 2,635.43 | 171.99 |
| Pittsfield, Mass. | 1,409.14 | 1,487.02 | 77.88 | Perth Amboy, N. J. | 2,172.80 | 2,241.76 | 68.96 |
| White Plains, N. Y. | 2,589.86 | 3,403.97 | 814.11 | Orange, N. J. | 2,009.76 | 2,639.02 | 629.26 |
| New Brunswick, N. J. | 1,917.79 | 2,299.46 | 381.67 | Brookline, Mass. | 2,271.47 | 2,331.23 | 59.76 |
| West Orange, N. J. | 2,024.02 | 2,061.86 | 37.84 | Hackensack, N. J. | 2,023.92 | 2,425.99 | 402.07 |
| West Springfield, Mass. | 1,676.48 | 1,777.81 | 101.33 | Braintree, Mass. | 1,480.03 | 1,631.61 | 151.58 |
| Northampton, Mass. | 1,472.80 | 1,670.23 | 197.43 | Englewood, N. J. | 2,224.18 | 2,396.19 | 172.01 |
| Long Branch, N. J. | 1,872.47 | 2,234.75 | 362.28 | Milford, Mass. | 1,395.61 | 1,502.40 | 106.79 |
| Norwood, Mass. | 1,643.91 | 1,822.44 | 178.53 | Gardner, Mass. | 1,533.41 | 1,621.86 | 88.45 |
| Adams, Mass. | 1,392.88 | 1,415.84 | 22.96 | Clinton, Mass. | 1,640.67 | 1,781.84 | 141.17 |
| MEAN | $1,910.76 | $2,171.87 | $261.11 | MEAN | $1,955.28 | $2,204.77 | $249.49 |

staff ratio when the twelve systems of each type of organization are considered as a whole, great similarity exists between the 6–3–3 and the 8–4 systems both as to actual and as to relative salaries in grades 7 to 9.  The mean salary in grades K to 6 in the 6–3–3 systems is $1,910.76 and in the 8–4 systems only slightly higher, $1,955.28.  Likewise in grades 7 to 9 the mean salary in the 6–3–3 systems is slightly lower than in the 8–4 systems, $2,171.87 as compared with $2,204.77.  When 7 to 9 costs are related to K to 6 costs, it will be noted that the mean average salaries in grades 7 to 9 exceed those in grades K to 6 by $261.11 in the 6–3–3 systems and $249.49 in the 8–4.  That is, whereas actual salaries are higher in the 8–4 systems than in the 6–3–3 in grades 7 to 9, the reverse is true of 7 to 9 salaries as related to K to 6 salaries, the variation between grade groups being slightly higher in the 6–3–3 systems than in the 8–4.

It appears then from Tables 36 and 37 that the similarity in actual and relative costs for the major item, instructional salaries, in grades 7 to 9 in the two types of organization is determined by similarity in pupil-teacher ratios and in average salaries paid the instructional staff.  It requires but one more step to indicate the relative importance of these two items.  Grades 7 to 9 in the twelve 6–3–3 systems could dispense with 103.53 teachers if they had the same pupil-staff ratio as grades K to 6.  If this number is multiplied by $2,171.87, the average salary paid in these twelve junior high schools, the result is $224,853.70, the amount that would be saved if there were the same number of pupils per teacher in grades 7 to 9 as in grades K to 6, salaries being maintained on the present junior high school level.  This would amount to a saving of $10.22 per pupil.  If, on the other hand, the pupil-teacher ratio is left undisturbed but junior high school salaries are reduced to the elementary level, the amount saved will be $253,263.64 (the present number of teachers, 969.95, multiplied by the difference in average salaries, $261.11).  This would be a saving of $11.51 per pupil.

In the twelve 8–4 systems if the pupil-teacher ratio of grades 7 to 9 is raised to the level of the lower grades, there would be 129.37 fewer teachers needed.  This number multiplied by $2,204.77, the average salary in these grades, gives a result of $285,231.09, a saving of $12.33 per pupil.  If the salaries in grades 7 to 9 are reduced to the elementary level but the pupil-teacher ratio remains the same, the amount saved would be $247,030.48 (the present number of teachers, 994.15, multiplied by $249.49, the difference in average salaries). This would lessen costs $10.68 per pupil.

It is apparent then that salaries are a slightly more important factor than pupil-staff ratio in explaining the difference in instructional costs between grades 7 to 9 and K to 6 in the twelve 6–3–3 systems, $11.51 per pupil compared with $10.22; but that in the 8–4 systems pupil-staff ratio is the more important factor, $12.33 per pupil compared with $10.68 per pupil. These differences probably are too slight, however, to warrant the conclusion that 6–3–3 systems generally tend to pay higher salaries in grades 7 to 9 as compared with grades K to 6 than do the 8–4 systems, and that 8–4 systems generally tend to have fewer pupils per teacher in grades 7 to 9 as compared with grades K to 6. A safer conclusion would seem to be that these slight differences are due to chance and that while two other groups of systems would probably show approximately the same results the slight differences might be reversed. In fact, if the weighted average is used instead of giving equal weight to the twelve systems of each group, it is found that in the 8–4 systems salaries rather than pupil-teacher ratio constitute the most important item but that salaries remain slightly more important in the 6–3–3 systems than pupil-teacher ratio.

It should be noted at this point that adding $10.22 and $11.51 (the savings to grades 7 to 9 in the 6–3–3 systems if pupil-staff ratio and instructional costs were on the K to 6 level) does not produce $21.21, the mean excess of instructional salaries in grades 7 to 9 over those in K to 6 (see Table 32). This is because the two factors are not additive, as is explained in Chapter V, since the importance of each factor in determining cost differences is measured as it operates with the other.

Reference to Tables 34 and 35 indicates that in the 6–3–3 systems instruction salaries account for 78.0 per cent of the differences in per pupil costs between grades 7 to 9 and K to 6 and in the 8–4 systems 76.8 per cent. If to these percentages there are added the percentages of the difference due to instructional costs other than salaries and to operation (two other items showing similar percentages in both types of organization), the result is a total of 92.4 per cent in the 6–3–3 systems and 92.5 per cent in the 8–4. In other words, great similarity exists between the two types of organization in the per pupil cost differences between grades 7 to 9 and K to 6 for instruction salaries, instruction other than salaries, and operation, and these three items constitute over 92 per cent of the total difference between grades K to 6 and 7 to 9 in the 6–3–3 and 8–4 systems. While the analysis of expenditures in terms of character classification has indicated that cost variations between grades K to 6 and 7 to 9 in both 6–3–3 and 8–4 organizations are primarily due to two causes, the ratio of pupils to staff members and the salaries paid to staff members, little attention has been given to the fundamental features of junior high school education and how they affect these two major cost determinants. These features and their cost implications are given consideration in the next chapter.

# IX

# Cost of the Standard Junior High School

THE first three phases of this study reported in the previous chapters have presented data bearing upon the cost of education in one hundred seven 6–3–3 systems in six eastern states, in certain 6–3–3 and 8–4 systems in Massachusetts, and in twelve selected 6–3–3 and twelve selected 8–4 systems. These data are reported with but little reference to the educational services offered other than that certain of the systems are 6–3–3 and others 8–4 in organization. It has, however, been pointed out repeatedly by educators that junior high schools are so variable in nature that one can attach but little importance, from the standpoint of educational service, to the mere statement that a system is of the 6–3–3 rather than of the 8–4 type. In spite of the fact that there has been defined and described a "standard" junior high school which comprehends a considerable array of ideal features and functions, there is far from complete agreement as to exactly what constitutes this standard junior high school. However, what constitutes ideal junior high school education is probably agreed upon as much as what constitutes ideal elementary or senior high school education.

The cost data reported in the previous chapters might be related to the standard junior high school in several ways. One way would be to set up a comprehensive check list of junior high school features and to check against this list the features provided by the 6–3–3 systems reported in this investigation. Another method would be to describe the educational programs of a number of the 6–3–3 systems for which detailed cost data are available. By either of these methods various types of junior high school programs of education might be associated with costs, but it would be difficult, if not impossible, to trace the influence of *each* feature on expenditures. Therefore it seems desirable in this last phase of the investigation to use a third method—to analyze, feature by feature, the cost implications of standard junior high

school education.   After this main purpose of the fourth phase
has been accomplished, the question may then be raised whether
or not the twelve selected 6–3–3 systems included in this investigation are spending enough to provide the desirable features of the
standard junior high school.   That is, there is no assumption
here that the failure of a system to be "standard" in certain respects is traceable entirely to costs.   Too often there has been a
strong belief that if costs are high enough the ideal features must
be present, and the allied belief that if costs are low the standard
features cannot be present.

Although an attempt is made to discuss the cost implications
of each of the features of the standard junior high school, stress
is laid upon those features most directly associated with pupil-
teacher ratio and salaries, since these two items account for the
major part of the cost differences which exist between grades 7
to 9 and K to 6 in junior high school systems.

The first problem is to determine the features of the standard
junior high school.   No attempt is made here to set up desirable
features differing greatly from those indicated by specialists in
this field, but the attempt is made to determine a list upon which
there is fairly common agreement.

Smith, upon the basis of "the collective judgment of the fore-
most leaders in the junior high school movement,"[1] has drawn
up a list of the major functions of the reorganized school which
includes the desirable features by which the major purposes or
functions may be realized.   These important purposes and features
are as follows:

I. To provide a suitable educational environment for children approximately
   twelve to sixteen years of age, embracing
   A. An enlarged experience background, involving especially
      1. Enriched curricula and course of study.
      2. Improved facilities by way of laboratories, shops, libraries, assembly
         halls, and gymnasiums.
      3. Superior teachers, including a larger percentage of men.
      4. New methods of teaching and social control.
      5. A distinctive school atmosphere.
   B. Ample provision for common socialized integrating education.
   C. Abundant facilities for the progressive discovery and experimental direction
      of pupils' interests, aptitudes, and abilities, involving especially

[1]W. A., Smith, *The Junior High School*, pp. 203–204, The Macmillan Company, 1925.   In arriving at
his major purposes Smith draws from the opinions of Bennett, Bonser, Briggs, Bunker, Cox, Davis,
Francis, Horn, Inglis, Johnston, Jones, Judd, Koos, Snedden, Van Denburg, and West.

    1. Exploratory activities in varied occupational fields.
    2. General and survey courses in the major academic fields.
    3. Individual and social diagnoses.
    4. Flexibility in curriculum organization and administration.
    5. Educational and vocational guidance.
  D. Adequate provision for individual differences, involving especially
    1. Enriched curricular and extracurricular offerings.
    2. Opportunities for gradual curriculum differentiation.
    3. Flexibility in methods of promotion.
    4. Provision for varying rates of progress.
    5. Vocational training for those who must leave school early.
  E. Increased opportunities for genuine socialization, involving especially
    1. An adequate program of extracurricular activities.
    2. Extensive provision for pupil participation in school government.
II. To democratize the school system, through
  A. Provision for a gradual transition from elementary to secondary education in such matters as
    1. Content.
    2. Methods of teaching.
    3. Social and administrative control.
  B. The democratization of educational opportunities.
III. To effect economy of time in education, largely through
  A. The elimination of waste from the seventh, eighth, and ninth grades.

In the present study a rather sharp distinction is made between the features and the functions of the junior high school. Pioneer writers in the field of junior high school education, such as Briggs, Cox, Inglis, and Davis, have devoted considerable space to the purposes or functions. This is as it should be since it is necessary to know the functions or objectives of an institution, at least in part, before there can be any intelligent effort toward determining the features of such an institution. With the clearer statement of the special purposes, functions, and provinces of junior high school education, there has come an attempt to set up the features of this unit of education. Koos has stated that *"the heart of the junior-high-school problem is the adaptation of the features to the performance of the functions,"* indicating that it is only in terms of the peculiar functions of the junior high school that there may be determined and defended the "exclusion of a feature or a particular variation of a feature from the junior-high-school plan or the inclusion of one in it," or the choice "between two or more variations of the same feature."[2]

Too sharp a feature-function differentiation is arbitrary since

[2] L. V. Koos, *The Junior High School*, p. 130, Enlarged Edition, Ginn and Company, 1927.

any adequate treatment of junior high school education must involve both the ends sought as well as the means of attaining them.   However, it is with means, or features that costs are primarily concerned, rather than with the ends, or functions to be performed.   This may be illustrated by the "peculiar functions of the junior-high-school" as distinguished from the "features" by Koos.   He lists the following as functions.[3]

1. Realizing a democratic school system through
    a) Retention of pupils.
    b) Economy of time.
    c) Recognition of individual differences.
    d) Exploration and guidance.
    e) Beginnings of vocational education.
2. Recognizing the nature of the child at adolescence.
3. Providing conditions for better teaching.
4. Securing better scholarship.
5. Improving the disciplinary situation and socializing opportunities.

It will be seen at once that the majority of these functions are in general terms and do not lend themselves readily to cost analysis. However, these functions, in the opinion of Koos, are best attained by a careful consideration of such features as (1) grades included in the junior high school; (2) the requirements of admission; (3) the program of studies provided; (4) ability grouping; (5) departmentalization; (6) the plan of promotion; (7) methods of instruction; (8) the advisory or adjustment system; (9) the social organization; (10) the staff provided; (11) housing and equipment provided.

The majority of these are specific items to be decided in the light of the functions of the junior high school, and decisions as to features such as these determine the junior high school set-up which must in large measure determine junior high school costs.

The following descriptive list of features of the standard junior high school is given not as a comprehensive and inclusive array of the elements of ideal junior high school education, but as a minimum list for the purpose of opening up in a general way the issues of cost.   Error in the inclusion of an item which does not to-day meet general approval, or in the omission of an item generally held desirable will not greatly affect the discussion here since the purpose is not to show with scientific precision what the standard junior high school must cost, but rather to indicate the

[3]Koos, *op. cit.*, p. 131.

place of financial support in providing for the features of ideal junior high school education. Nevertheless it is believed that many specialists in the reorganization movement will agree that the junior high school should be characterized by the following features:

1. The inclusion of grades 7 to 9. (Some modification, such as the 6–6 type, would probably be held desirable for smaller communities, but this investigation is limited to the larger systems.)

2. Some degree of departmentalization; complete in all grades of the junior high school if there has been preparation in the upper grades of the elementary school, or partial in grade 7 and increasing in grades 8 and 9 if there has been no preparation for departmentalization in the grades below.

3. An advisory-counseling-adjustment program which shall extend to the choice of a curriculum and to vocational interests as well as to social, recreational, and disciplinary problems.

4. Promotion by subject rather than by grade.

5. Admission based not rigidly on the completion of the sixth grade, but in some instances giving weight to social and physical maturity, and chronological age, as well as to achievement in school subject-matter.

6. A system of collateral student activities which shall be so organized and so sponsored as to be educationally effective.

7. Provision for individual differences by means of opportunities for gradual curriculum differentiation, enriched curricular offerings, or by some method of varying the rates of progress.

8. A program of studies made up of constants and variables in which the constants are required of all pupils in each grade and which provide the minimum essentials for the attainment of the major educational objectives and such other materials as may be commonly useful for all pupils as exploratory or broadening and finding courses, and in which the variable content shall include the materials necessary for differentiated exploration, and for some recognition of the vocational as well as the recreational aim.

9. Methods of instruction which show a departure from the constant use of the conventional recitation plan and an acceptance of some of the newer techniques of instruction, particularly those which are adapted to the purposes of junior high school education.

10. A staff consisting of both men and women who have not only something of a background in the whole reorganization movement and are alert to its purposes, but who are adequately trained in the content and methods of their special subjects of instruction, and who show some degree of adaptability to the direction of boys and girls of junior high school age.

11. Buildings and equipment of such a nature as to facilitate the attainment of the junior high school purposes.

To the extent that these are the essential features of the junior high school they will determine in large measure the essential costs of the standard junior high school.

The first feature indicated as essential to the realization of the junior high school aim is that of the inclusion of grades 7 to 9 in the junior high school unit.[4]  In some instances the 6–3–3 method of grouping grades might prove more costly than the 8–4 method since the former demands three distinct units of organization in place of the two which obtain in the 8–4 systems.  Any tendency to increase the number of organizational units might tend to increase costs due to smaller units of operation as opposed to larger. This third unit would require an additional principal or principals, probably added clerical aid and perhaps more supervisors.  Likewise, the creation of this third unit might make impossible a certain interlocking of the work of teachers which is successfully carried out between the upper grades of the eight-year elementary school and between the four years of the regular high school, thus requiring more teachers than would be needed under the two-unit plan.  Some or all of these things would probably happen in the smaller communities.  But in the larger communities such a situation need not arise.  The critical issue here is one of the concentration of pupils and therefore the centralization of effort in junior high school centers.  In fact, so vital is this issue of the centralization and consolidation of junior high school education that it appears at times to transcend all other issues in determining cost.

The 6–3–3 method of grouping grades inherently aids and facilitates the concentration of pupils in grades 7 and 8, whereas the 8–4 plan as it functions to-day retards and hinders it.  As has already been indicated (see Chapter VI) the tapering off in enrollment in the upper grades coupled with the tendency to continue classes from the lower grades through grades 7 and 8 has a tendency in 8–4 systems to decrease class-size in these latter grades. On the other hand, when the organization of the elementary school is disrupted at the end of the sixth grade, as in the 6–3–3 systems, and the pupils are thrown into a new organization, an opportune time has arisen so to concentrate the enrollment from two or more elementary schools into one unit as to insure that each class in each subject will start out in the seventh grade at maximum size. This will tend to overcome the higher per pupil costs incident to

[4]The discussion of this point does not involve the question of various types of junior high school systems (for example 6–3–3 as opposed to 6–2–4) but the question of the 6–3–3 grouping of grades as opposed to the 8–4.

the tapering-off process in class-size which so often accompanies the situation where grades 7 and 8 are maintained as an integral part of the elementary unit. Since the 6–3–3 method of grade grouping requires a new organization at the end of the sixth grade, it may on the whole be said to facilitate the concentration of pupils in grades 7 and 8.[5]

The 6–3–3 type of organization not only facilitates consolidation of pupils in fairly large junior high school units, but it requires that this be accomplished if costs are to be kept down, because of the introduction of a great number of variables into the program of studies. That is, when all subjects are required of all pupils there need be less consolidation of pupils to insure that classes will be of maximum size. But the introduction of many elective subjects which tend to divide pupils into small groups makes it imperative, from a cost standpoint, that there be enough concentration of pupils into one junior high school unit to insure that the classes in variables as well as in constants are at a maximum. The necessity for this will be discussed in more detail in connection with the cost implications of the junior high school program of studies.

There are probably no issues more vital to costs in the whole

[5]Although the 6–3–3 type of organization tends to facilitate consolidation and although in common practice the tendency is to combine the upper grades of several elementary schools into one junior high school unit, nevertheless in many cases the concentration of pupils has not been sufficient. Undoubtedly the tendency of some 6–3–3 systems to show higher costs is due to the lack of consolidation. This situation was encountered a number of times during the present investigation and is well illustrated by a 6–3–3 system in a community of a little over 40,000 population. Although this city is particularly compact, five separate and distinct junior high school units are provided. Per pupil costs in grades 7 to 9 in this system were found to be almost double what they were in a neighboring 8–4 system. Part of this was due to a generally higher salary level in the 6–3–3 organization. But much of it was due to the very considerable difference in class-size between the two organizations. Because of lack of sufficient enrollment in several of the junior high school units of the 6–3–3 system, class-size in constant subjects was small and in many variable subjects it was very small. That is, when the pupils in grades 7 to 9 were divided into five separate groups or schools it left the enrollment of several of them so small that classes even in required subjects were small, and when this enrollment was divided between a variety of elective subjects many of the classes were so small as hardly to be justified. One of the five junior high schools employed a printing instructor at a salary considerably above the average paid in the system and yet the enrollment in his classes ranged from four to nine. Such a condition results in extremely high per pupil costs. Likewise, the enrollment in many classes in the foreign languages, in the practical arts, and in commercial work averaged so low as to result in inordinately high per pupil costs.

In an effort to discover why there were five junior high schools in the 6–3–3 system it was found the city had grown up in five more or less distinct centers or communities and that at the time of reorganization each had demanded its own junior high school unit. It would seem that the extremely high per pupil costs shown by this junior high school system should be considered not as a legitimate charge arising from conditions which are inherent in junior high school education but as a charge against the desire of the people of this community to have their educational service in close proximity to their homes rather than concentrated in one or two junior high school centers.

junior high school situation than this question of the consolidation of pupils. Probably it is not too much to say that when junior high school education is not at least reasonably centralized it must inevitably cost more than traditional education, but that when it is well concentrated it *may* cost less. More concentration does not insure low costs but it does create a situation which makes low costs possible. It does so largely because of another feature of the standard junior high school, the program of studies.

Koos has stated "that to provide satisfactory junior-high-school education with all that this implies in elective curricula . . . must cost more than to provide the kind of training characteristic of the upper elementary grades . . ."[6]  Other writers in this field have taken a somewhat similar view. Such a position apparently has been substantiated by several early investigations which report higher per pupil costs by subjects in grades 7 and 8 in junior high than in traditional schools. Moreover, it is usually held that the fact that in traditional systems the per pupil costs are higher in the high school than in the elementary school is partly due to the program of studies including such matters as elective subjects and elective curricula. Nevertheless, it is desirable to examine the reorganized program of studies for any inherent features which might require higher costs than those of the traditional program.

The program of studies may influence per pupil costs in three major ways. First, it may affect class-size. Second, it may affect the instructional load carried by teachers and the subject load carried by pupils. Third, it may require a staff of such a nature as to modify salaries. It is apparent that if the standard junior high school program of studies requires smaller classes, it will be responsible for increased per pupil costs. Likewise, if the program necessitates the carrying of more subjects by the pupil but fewer periods by the teacher, it will cause higher costs per pupil. And finally if the program of studies requires a staff which may be provided only at a higher salary level, it is obvious that this must result in increased per pupil costs.

An enriched program of studies may indirectly affect costs in other ways. It may, for example, create the necessity for a considerable non-teaching staff which would increase per pupil costs. However, this and certain other similar possibilities will be dis-

[6] Koos, *op. cit.*, p. 107.

cussed in connection with other features of the standard junior high school.

There appears to be no valid reason for classes in many constant subjects to be smaller in the enriched curriculum than in the traditional. In such subjects as general social science, general mathematics, and English, for example, class-size may be kept at a maximum in the junior high school. If forty pupils can be taught traditional eighth-grade arithmetic effectively by one teacher at one time in the traditional school, forty pupils can be taught general mathematics effectively by one teacher at one time in the junior high school.

It is true that there are some constants in the junior high school, such as household arts and manual arts (often required of all pupils in grade 7), which are usually considered as inherently requiring small classes. Since there is little evidence to show either that classes in these subjects should be smaller than classes in academic subjects or how much smaller they should be, it is not possible to indicate how costs would be affected by the ideal situation. That, however, is not material to the discussion here since these practical arts subjects have come to be a part of the program of studies of 8–4 schools to a very considerable extent. Very few school systems in communities of more than 5,000 population fail to provide these courses in grades 7 and 8. If the teaching of such subjects does actually result in appreciably higher per pupil costs, these higher costs are a charge against evolving programs of education everywhere and not against junior high school education alone.

The cost effect of variables is more complex. But almost immediately one may question whether they are so costly as at first they appear. The ninth grade variables may be practically eliminated as a factor of cost since there are often as many electives in grade 9 in the traditional program as in the reorganized program. Likewise, variables in grade 7 are of little importance since the standard junior high school program of education calls for few if any electives in the seventh grade. This leaves only the variables in the eighth grade as factors which may from the standpoint of elective subjects peculiarly affect costs in the junior high school.

It is not known that the variables in the eighth grade of junior high schools must show higher per pupil costs than the subjects offered in the traditional school.   Nor is it clear whether higher costs for variables have been postulated because of the inherent nature of the subjects or because such subjects are elective rather than required, or both.   These questions must be decided largely by examining the variables most often recommended for the eighth grade and by examining the conditions under which they are offered.   In order to carry on differentiated exploration and to provide for vocational and recreational aims it is usually recommended that such subjects as foreign languages, household arts (clothing and foods), shop (woodwork, metal work, home mechanics), music, commercial work, art, and printing be included in the eighth grade program of studies as variables.

Although objective evidence is not available there seems to be nothing inherent in the nature of the majority of these subjects requiring or even making desirable smaller classes than obtain in subjects of the traditional program.   Foreign languages do not seem to require small classes for efficient work and the reason commonly offered for few pupils per class in these subjects is that relatively few pupils elect them.   This, likewise, appears to be true of the commercial work and the fine arts offered to boys and girls in the eighth grade.   It was found during this investigation that those commercial teachers in junior high schools who were responsible for as many as forty pupils at one time did not feel that the quality of their work was impaired because of class-size. In fact, some teachers felt that large classes were conducive to a type of discipline highly desirable in commercial work or business training.   The art ordinarily offered in junior high school is seldom highly individualized; hence there appears to be little reason why art classes should be restricted to numbers below those in academic subjects.

The practical arts—various kinds of shop work for boys and home economics for girls—have apparently in both theory and practice called for smaller classes.   Just how small these classes should be for the greatest efficiency is not known.   It was found in the present investigation that classes of thirty in woodwork were being carried on with apparently the same efficiency and dispatch as classes with less than half that number.   However, opinion seems to run strongly in favor of small classes.   Nevertheless, this is not a material issue here since manual arts and household arts are offered in the eighth grade in 8–4 systems to about the same extent as in 6–3–3. In fact, these subjects are often required in the eighth grade in the traditional systems, whereas they are usually elective in the reorganized systems; therefore, if such subjects require smaller classes, they will tend to raise costs more in 8–4 than in 6–3–3 systems since they affect all pupils (being required) in the former systems and only a part of them (being elective) in the latter. It is likely that those who do not elect the practical arts will elect a foreign language or some such subject in which numbers are not so restricted as in manual and household arts. On the other hand, there is a greater tendency to offer metal work, home mechanics, and similar work to boys in junior high schools than to those in the traditional schools. To the extent that these subjects require fewer pupils per class than is required in the subjects which they replace, costs in the reorganized system will tend to be higher than in the unreorganized.

It was found that printing was the one subject which apparently everywhere, under all conditions, had small classes. An attempt was made to find the reason for this. It was discovered that because of the space required and the expense of equipment only a small number could be accommodated at one time. From the standpoint of instruction there appears to be no reason why double the usual number cannot be accommodated in one class. It is poor economy to cut down on space and equipment only to employ a man with an above-average-salary to instruct three or four classes, of six or eight boys each, in the rudiments of printing. It is doubtful if any junior high school purpose will justify such an expenditure. It should be pointed out, however, that even at its worst the printing situation is not as costly as it appears, because in practically every case printing classes are partly self-supporting and in some advanced classes are entirely so.

Until more evidence has been presented, one may entertain considerable doubt as to whether the variables offered in the reorganized program of studies require, because of their inherent nature, substantially fewer pupils per class than do the subjects in traditional schools of the size included in this investigation. If, then, variables in the junior high school show higher costs than subjects in the traditional school or higher costs than constant subjects in the junior high school, it must be largely because such subjects are elective rather than required.

Classes in the junior high school are smaller in elective than in required subjects apparently because class-size in the latter is more controllable. The class-size of each section in English, for example, may be arranged at or near the maximum before the opening of school in the fall. The numbers in the in-coming eighth-grade class may be estimated from the records of the preceding spring term, since it is known that except for a few irregulars all these pupils will take English. But there is less certainty about elective subjects even though it is now a common practice to have a tentative registration for the fall term before school is dismissed in the spring. Far more contributory, however, to small classes in variables than are the uncertainties of enrollment at the time of schedule-making is the fact that many school administrators have not set themselves sufficiently to the problem of obviating small classes in elective subjects. Seemingly the constants set the pace; if they show large classes, things are not far wrong. Evidently the fact that a subject is variable justifies a small class-size.

The key to this difficulty of small classes in elective subjects is the consolidation of pupils in larger junior high school units. Where numbers are concentrated, many of the administrative difficulties incident to the consistent maintenance of large classes will tend to disappear. It is, for example, obvious that some eighth grade classes must show small numbers when a junior high school with an enrollment inadequate for such a program offers art, music, French, German, Latin, foods, clothing, household management, home nursing, woodwork, metal work, electricity, home mechanics, and printing (which is not uncommon), each pupil being able to elect only four to six periods of this work per week. No matter what administrative manipulations are resorted to, there will not be enough pupils to fill all of these classes to a desirable size. Nor does it matter whether this junior high school is in a small community or in a large city; if the unit of junior high school education is small, it is inevitable that some elective classes (if electives are offered on a large scale) will also be small. On the other hand, elective subjects may be increased in number in proportion to consolidation without endangering class-size.

Difficulties in schedule-making are sometimes offered as justification for running several classes in the same elective subject at different periods of the day in order to accommodate all pupils desiring the subject, whereas one class would often be sufficient purely from the standpoint of numbers. This difficulty usually disappears when the enrollment is large. The mere fact that the concentration of numbers requires more than one section in many of the subjects will often fulfill the demand for having a subject at various periods of the day. One factor which has at times complicated the making of schedules and has resulted in smaller elective classes is ability grouping. When individual differences are recognized almost wholly by segregating pupils rigidly in ability groups, a situation may arise which is much like having several schools within one school; that is, if the groups are sharply differentiated, they move as more or less separate and distinct units, even though they are integral parts of the same organization. This segregation, when applied to elective subjects, has the same effect as lack of sufficient enrollment. It is usual in practice, however, to disregard ability grouping to some extent when placing pupils in variable subjects. Furthermore, the fact that there is some correlation between ability and type of work elected tends to smooth out this difficulty.

However one may look at the situation, there appear no reasons whatever for class-size in elective subjects being smaller than in required, except that the control of numbers is often exceedingly difficult in elective subjects. And the key to this control seems to be largely the size of the junior high school unit, although in some instances it appears that administrators have not been properly diligent in seeking other plans to keep class-size in variables at a maximum.

It is hardly possible to over-estimate the necessity for constant attention to class-size if per pupil costs are to be kept down. Previous chapters have revealed the important effect of class-size and pupil-staff ratio on per pupil costs. It is evident, therefore, that class-size in variable subjects is one of the vital points of attack in keeping down school costs. The argument is not so much to increase the maximum size of classes, although because of recent financial pressure there is a tendency to do this, but rather to see that all, or at least most, classes carry their maximum load. The situation is not greatly relieved by putting forty or more pupils in English and social science classes, and at the same time allowing less than half this number in many variable classes.

Thus far the discussion of the probable influences on cost of the standard junior high school program of studies has been restricted largely to class-size. There is, however, a second factor which at times becomes of considerable importance. This, as has already been indicated, is the amount of work carried by the pupils, designated as pupil load, and the amount of work for which teachers are responsible, usually called teaching load. Either or both of these may be incident to reorganization from the traditional to the junior high school program of studies. It will be seen as the discussion progresses that this factor involves another feature of the standard junior high school, that of departmentalization.

In the upper as well as in the lower grades in some traditional systems, although common practice to-day tends away from such a situation, one teacher is responsible for one class from the opening of school in the morning to dismissal time in the afternoon. She teaches all subjects from arithmetic to art (perhaps relieved a period or two per week by a "traveling teacher" of such subjects as music and nature study). In systems of this kind class-size is practically synonymous with pupil-teacher ratio. In the less traditional 8–4 systems some degree of departmentalization is often introduced; in many instances there is complete departmentalization in grades 7 and 8. But the circumstances under which it operates vary considerably from system to system. In some systems the loads of the pupil and teacher continue to be practically the same, even though no one teacher is entirely responsible for one class. In other systems the teaching load is reduced, although the pupil load is maintained as before or perhaps is increased. In such a case, although class-size is not changed, the pupil-teacher ratio in the whole system is reduced, and per pupil costs for instructional salaries are therefore increased.

When traditional schools reorganize to the junior high school system, departmentalization, unless it is already in use, is almost invariably one of the major changes accomplished. But the resultant relationship between pupil and teacher load varies greatly from system to system. It is not uncommon for junior high school pupils to carry a load of forty periods per week (including regularly scheduled periods for guidance or adjustment, clubs, assemblies, and similar non-academic work) while the average teaching load may be only twenty-five periods per week, or less. When such a situation is compared with a traditional-school situation in which one teacher is responsible for one class during the entire school day, assuming the same class-size and the same salary schedule, it will be found that the per pupil costs for instructional salaries are 37.5 per cent higher in the junior high school. If forty periods per week per pupil and twenty-five periods per week per teacher describe the average junior high school program while equal pupil and teacher loads in terms of periods[7] are common practice in the traditional system, here is a factor tending toward sharply higher per pupil costs in the former systems.

Writers in this field have reported common practices and have made certain recommendations relative to junior high school teaching load and pupil load. They have not, however, associated the two factors, nor noted to what a considerable extent they determine pupil-teacher ratio and, therefore, per pupil costs. The problem cannot be definitely settled here. Common practice is so variable in this matter that little of value may be drawn from it; and the approach by way of what is demanded by the standard junior high school is equally difficult since few authorities in this field have ventured more than the reporting of common practices and the making of general recommendations. However, for the purpose of opening up the problem, there is reported in Table 38 a junior high school program of studies which was proposed by the executive curriculum committee of junior high schools of Springfield, Massachusetts.[8]

The Springfield program of studies is reported here, not because it conforms to all the standards set up for the ideally reorganized program,[9] but because it shows what may be done in the way of balancing teacher and pupil load while still approaching that which is standard in junior high school education. It will be noted in this program that a total of twenty-five periods (which in this case also amounts to twenty-five hours) is required of each pupil in each of the junior high school grades per week and that these twenty-five periods account for the entire classroom school week of each pupil.

[7] Teaching load is used in its narrow sense in this discussion and pertains to the number of classes taught daily or weekly. Other factors, such as the personality of the class, the number of different preparations for class work required daily, the amount of clerical work connected with the teaching process, extra-classroom school duties, and certain civic and social demands enter into the situation and must be recognized in some manner.

[8] The committee recommended that this program become effective in September, 1932.

[9] Several features might not be acceptable to all authorities in the junior high school field. For example, little time has been set aside specifically for guidance and adjustment—although this might be defended if the liberal time given to supervised study, half of each class hour, is used in part for counseling purposes. Likewise, there may be a lack of regularly scheduled time devoted to club work, assemblies, or collateral student activities.

According to Note 2 (Table 38) the load of teachers of art, home economics, manual arts, music, and physical education is identical with the pupil load, twenty-five periods per week.  According to Note 1 the load of academic teachers, twenty-two periods per week

TABLE 38

PROPOSED PROGRAM OF STUDIES FOR JUNIOR HIGH SCHOOLS, SPRINGFIELD, MASSACHUSETTS, TO BECOME EFFECTIVE SEPTEMBER 1, 1932

*A total of 25 hours per week of required and elective subjects required of each pupil in each grade*

| GRADE 7 | | GRADE 8 | | GRADE 9 | |
|---|---|---|---|---|---|
| *Required Subjects* | *Hours per Week* | *Required Subjects* | *Hours per Week* | *Required Subjects* | *Hours per Week* |
| Home Room Period and Guidance (15 min. per day) | | Home Room Period and Guidance (15 min. per day) | | Home Room Period (15 min. per day) | |
| English | 5 | English | 5 | English | 4 |
| Mathematics | 4 | Mathematics | 4 | Guidance | 1 |
| Nature Study and Health | 2 | Nature Study and Health | 2 | Science | 4 |
| Social Studies | 5 | Social Studies | 5 | Social Studies | 4 |
| Art | 2 | Assembly | 1 | Assembly | 1 |
| Assembly | 1 | Music | 1 | Physical Education | 2 |
| Home Economics (Girls) | 2 | Physical Education | 2 | Study or Club Period | 1 |
| Foods—7B | | Study or Club Period | 1 | | 17 |
| Clothing—7A | | | 21 | | |
| Manual Arts (Boys) | 2 | | | | |
| Woodwork—7B | | | | | |
| Metal Work—7A | | *Elective Subjects* (4 hours) | | *Elective Subjects* (8 hours) | |
| Music | 1 | | | | |
| Physical Education | 2 | Art | 2 | Algebra | 4 |
| Study or Club Period | 1 | Foreign Language | 4 | Art | 2 |
| | 25 | French, German, Latin | | Foreign Language | 4 |
| | | Home Economics (Girls) | 2–4 | French, German, Latin | |
| | | Foods—8B | | Home Economics (Girls) | 2–4 |
| | | Clothing—8A | | Foods—9B | |
| | | Manual Arts (Boys) | 2–4 | Clothing—9A | |
| | | Electricity and Home Mechanics—8B | | Introduction to Business | 4 |
| | | Printing—8A | | Manual Arts (Boys) | 2–4–8 |
| | | Music | 2 | Electricity and Home Mechanics | |
| | | | 25 | Mechanical Drawing | |
| | | | | Metal Work | |
| | | | | Printing | |
| | | | | Woodwork | |
| | | | | Music | 2 |
| | | | | | 25 |

NOTES:
1.  Load of Academic Teachers, 22 periods per week, plus a home room.
2.  Load of Teachers of Art, Home Economics, Manual Arts, Music, and Physical Education, 25 periods per week.
3.  No class in any subject is to be organized with fewer than 20 pupils.
4.  In academic subjects the class hour is to be broken up into two periods, each 30 minutes in length. One period is to be used for recitation, the other for supervised study.

plus a home room, is somewhat less than the pupil load. There is, however, practically no difference between the academic teaching load and the pupil load. In the first place, the academic teachers are also responsible for one period of club or study, making their load twenty-three periods. In the second place, the one assembly per week is a period for which the teachers are not responsible as a part of their regular twenty-five periods, so that from the standpoint of the teachers' time the pupil load is only twenty-four periods instead of twenty-five. In summary, then, the load of pupils is twenty-four periods per week; the load of academic teachers, twenty-three periods; and the load of non-academic teachers, twenty-five periods. It appears, therefore, that for this junior high school, teacher and pupil loads are practically identical, and the pupil-teacher ratio is the same as average class-size.

The Springfield program of studies illustrates a junior high school which requires no more teachers from the standpoint of balance between pupil and teacher load than the most conservative of traditional schools. In fact, since city school systems commonly tend toward departmentalization in the upper grades in 8–4 organizations (in which the pupil load, measured by periods or hours, sometimes exceeds the teacher load) the Springfield program tends to have lower per pupil costs than many traditional systems. No final word can be offered in this matter until there is a more scientific basis upon which to determine teaching load and pupil load. Meanwhile, those interested in the reorganized program of education should realize that pupil and teacher loads are two related factors to which per pupil costs are astonishingly sensitive.

A third factor which may be associated with the program of studies and one which is itself a feature of the standard junior high school is the staff. While all the elements which together constitute the reorganized school must enter into a determination of the ideal junior high school staff, none of these elements is so important as the program of studies. On the other hand, probably no feature is so important as the staff in determining the successful functioning of this program. Briggs has stated:[10]

The success of any educational institution depends primarily on its teachers. Even when the purposes are clear, the courses of study well determined, the prin-

[10]T. H. Briggs, *The Junior High School*, p. 210, Houghton Mifflin Company, 1920.

ciples of discipline developed by experience, and traditions established, teachers make or mar the success of the organization. In the junior high school, where many details are relatively new and where in consequence much pioneering must be done, the importance of the teachers is correspondingly magnified.

Koos, likewise, believes[11] that

In spite of all the importance that may be ascribed to other features of the junior high school, the supreme place of properly qualified teachers and principals in effecting thoroughgoing reorganization cannot be gainsaid. It is not too much to say that if a staff meeting all desirable requirements could be secured, most of the remaining features would soon follow.

This dependence may be more readily appreciated if the properly qualified teacher is briefly described in terms of his relations to the features of the new institution. . . . Since it is the teacher who presents the materials of the program, he should have sufficient ability in the fields he is teaching to assemble and organize them. . . . He must be equipped to teach by the newer types of method, invoking the use of directed study, project, socialization, and individualization. . . . Adequately to administer all the features named he should also measure up on what Gosling refers to as the "moral requirements" of the junior-high-school teacher, namely, understanding of and sympathy with adolescent boys and girls. . . .

Smith in commenting on the ideal staff for the junior high school states:[12]

It is quite obvious that only a well trained teacher can function effectively with reference to the major purposes of the junior high school. Exploration and guidance, which make such heavy demands upon the junior high school teacher, are in the very nature of the case quite out of the question without a thoroughgoing grasp of subject-matter, a keen understanding of children, and a good command of educational practices. In addition the junior high school teacher needs a large fund of general knowledge extending far beyond his own special field.

A review of the literature pertaining to the desirable staff for the standard junior high school seems to indicate that there is at least an approach to the ideal when teachers (1) have a general but substantial background in the purposes and peculiar functions of the junior high school; (2) are well trained in the special subjects to be taught and in the special teaching techniques or methods best adapted to them and to the junior high school; (3) are equipped to handle or direct with a reasonable degree of skill certain special junior high school agencies of education, such as guidance and collateral student activities; (4) show some adaptation to the teaching of boys and girls of the junior high school age. It should be noted

[11]Koos, *op. cit.*, pp. 446–447.
[12]W. A. Smith, *The Junior High School*, p. 414, The Macmillan Company, 1925.

that these items are not intended as an inclusive list but rather as an indication of the unique kind of training a junior high school teacher should have.

Will it cost more to secure the services of a staff with the above equipment than it now costs to secure the services of teachers in grades 7 to 9 in the average 8–4 system in communities of more than 5,000 population? Those most familiar with the ramifications and hazards of salary issues probably would not attempt an answer, realizing that an adequate answer is not possible. On the other hand, the stress put upon salaries by writers in this field seems to indicate that, in the minds of many, adequate staffs mean higher salaries.

In the past the most difficult task faced by those who wished to secure junior high school teachers was the matter of supply. It was not so much a question of what must be paid to secure the services of a teacher for this new unit as it was a question of how the profession of junior high school teacher was to be created; there was no supply available at any price. One of the most interesting accounts of how this was accomplished is from Rochester, New York. The following is an extract from a report[13] made in 1923 on the work of the junior high schools of that city.

*The Teaching Staff.* The junior high school teachers have for the most part been selected from the upper grades of the grammar schools. One year before Washington Junior High School was opened, a series of Saturday Morning Institutes was begun. Classes were organized in Latin, German, English, Elementary Science, and Mathematics. These institutes were for applicants for teaching positions in the Academic Course. Specially trained teachers were available for the Commercial, Household, and Industrial Arts Courses. Saturday Morning Institutes, however, were organized and carried on through the year in these courses also, for the main purpose of outlining provisional courses of study.

Prior to the opening of the Jefferson Junior High School the University of Rochester offered courses in the organization, administration, and supervision of the junior high school, as well as courses dealing with the teaching of the various subjects. These courses were taken by those teachers who desired appointment as teachers in the Jefferson Junior High School. Upon the completion of the courses eligible lists were prepared and the teachers selected from these lists. The following factors were considered in securing the final rating: training, length of teaching experience, quality of service, personality, and rating in university extension courses.

For the Madison and Monroe Junior High Schools teachers were chosen from the upper grades of the city schools, from the high schools, and from outside the city,

---

[13]Board of Education, Rochester, New York (H. S. Weet, Superintendent), *The Junior High Schools of Rochester, New York*, p. 42.

only those best qualified as to preparation, experience, and personality being selected.

*University Courses.* In the fall of 1919 the University of Rochester and the Department of Public Instruction co-operated in offering special courses to all teachers who desired to become familiar with the work of junior high schools and junior high school grades. These courses carried college credit and provided special instruction in methods in all the academic subjects taught in the grades. The response of the teachers was most gratifying. The majority of those teaching in the 7th and 8th grades availed themselves of the opportunity to get instruction in the best methods of presenting the particular subject in which they were interested. These courses proved extremely valuable in preparing teachers to do their work under the new type of organization. An ever increasing number of teachers are availing themselves of this privilege of taking extension courses, the cost of which has been shared by the Board of Education. During the first semester of the year 1922–23, 439 teachers were enrolled in the various extension courses offered by the University of Rochester. In the second semester 312 teachers were enrolled.

The report states that teachers who were selected for the junior high school positions "from regular grade positions in the Rochester schools shall receive an initial salary of at least $100.00 in excess of what they would otherwise receive."[14] This seems to be a very slight differential and one which indicates that the greatest motive for preparation for junior high school teaching came from sources other than substantially increased salaries. The amount of the increase does not, however, exhibit all the facts in the situation. This $100.00 differential is on the position basis. Greater differences than this might appear because of preparation; that is, the concentration of better prepared teachers in the junior high school might have the result of increasing costs very materially aside from the position differential, since it is common practice to pay higher salaries for better preparation. Yet the very fact that the teachers were drawn largely from the elementary grades would result in a preparation status in the junior high school somewhat similar to that which had obtained in the upper grades before reorganization.

More important by far than financial encouragement appear to be the *means* by which an ambitious teacher might become well prepared for her new profession. The Rochester report has little to say of the motive but much to say of the provision of means by which teachers for this new unit might become trained. There is little indication of the inspirational but much of the definite plan in the Rochester situation.

[14]Board of Education, Rochester, New York, *op. cit.*, p. 45.

Because of the importance attributed to the salary level as a determinant of junior high school costs, considerable attention was directed to salaries during the present investigation.  Particularly important are certain facts relative to the relationships existing between salaries and preparation in the junior high school.  The personnel record cards of nine of the twelve 6–3–3 systems included in the third phase of this investigation were examined, as well as those in a number of other 6–3–3 systems.  The following facts pertinent at this point were discovered.  First, that in every system examined the junior high school teachers' training was nearer in amount to the senior high school teachers' than to the elementary.  Second, that the typical elementary teacher had two years of training above high school, the typical senior high school teacher had four years of training above high school, and in most instances it would be an error to say that there was a typical junior high school teacher from the standpoint of training.  Third, that while the years of training as well as the type of training of junior high school teachers showed a tremendous variation within the same system, the salaries of these teachers tended to be about equal. Often this is defended on the basis that those with little training have more experience.  However, the personnel cards show that much of this experience usually has been as an elementary teacher, not as a junior high school teacher.  In many respects the personnel cards of the average junior high school stand as an indictment of too great a dependence upon salaries alone as the means of securing desirable junior high school staffs.  When one finds, side by side in the same system, receiving the same salaries, a number of teachers with no special preparation whatsoever for their work and an equal number of other teachers who are well trained, it seems an indication that some plan other than position differentials in salaries must be adopted.

There is no intention to deny here that salaries are one of several valuable and definite means of securing a desirable school staff, particularly in competing with other communities for the services of teachers.  However, seemingly too often there has been a tendency to have faith in the payment of wages alone as the means of bringing to the junior high school a desirable staff.

The original question was whether or not the evidence indicated that a community could secure the services of teachers who in the main conform to the standards set up here at a salary level not

materially different from that of grades 7 to 9 in 8–4 systems in
communities of more than 5,000 population.   Several things would
tend toward an affirmative answer at present.   First, in 8–4 systems the salaries of teachers in grades 7 and 8 are usually higher
than the salaries of teachers in grades 1 to 6; this coupled with the
fact that salaries in grade 9 are almost invariably much higher than
in grades 1 to 6 means that salaries in grades 7 to 9 as a whole are
substantially higher than in grades 1 to 6 in the average traditional
system.   Hence a salary level in grades 7 to 9 in 6–3–3 systems
which is comparable to the salary level in these grades in 8–4 systems would put average junior high school salaries somewhat above
average salaries paid in grades 1 to 6, and thus eliminate competition from the lower grades.   Second, the payment of higher salaries
in grades 7 to 9 than in 1 to 6 (that is, position differential in salaries), when unsupported by other measures, has failed in the average junior high school to secure the services of an ideal staff.
There are at the present moment side by side in the same systems
many teachers with outstanding qualifications and equally as
many with apparently no preparation for the special work of the
junior high school.   Likewise, among different systems in the
same general localities there seems to be little relationship between
salaries and preparation.   Although the variation in the average
years of training of junior high school teachers is insignificant between the two systems in the New York metropolitan area examined in this investigation, the average salary variation is substantial between these same organizations.   Third, there is much
to indicate that at the present moment either actually or poten-
tially there is available a great supply of young men and women
who have or are willing to secure the preparation requisite for the
desirable junior high school teacher.   Seemingly there is a para-
doxical situation here; on the one hand the average junior high
school is inadequately staffed, and on the other, prospective teachers are warned that there is a tremendous over-supply of teachers in
practically all levels of work and that unless training institutions
curtail their numbers immediately there will be more serious un-
employment among teachers than among many other professions.
Evidently there is a question as to whether there does actually
exist an over-supply of genuinely desirable teachers on the junior
high school level.   Certainly if there is such an over-supply it has

accomplished little in the way of forcing up the preparation level of teachers. Nevertheless, whether the present supply is actual or only potential, if a definite stand were taken by communities, in the years immediately ahead the preparation level of junior high school teachers could probably be raised to conform more nearly to what is generally considered ideal. There seems no explanation for the present situation except that communities have for one reason or another protected the poorly prepared teacher in the junior high school from direct competition with those who are more adequately prepared, or at least against competition with many who are willing to become well prepared.

Certain other factors, on the contrary, would tend toward a negative answer to the original question. First, the level of salaries which would obtain in the junior high school if it were the same as now obtains in grades 7 to 9 in the traditional system would be below that of the senior high school and therefore, it has been urged, the latter would have a constant tendency to take the more successful teachers from the junior high school. Second, it is often contended that the level of salaries is lower than the income of many other professions and that the junior high school (or any other school unit) cannot hope to secure the services of the finest men and women unless salaries are higher. The degree to which this actually operates is not known. However, there is evidence that the salaries in the professions which at present attract the greatest numbers of women (such as nursing, library service, and social work) are lower than in junior high school teaching. And one wonders how much higher salaries would have to be in school work in order to attract great numbers of those men who now enter law, medicine, engineering, and architecture.

On the whole it seems that if the procuring of the services of the ideal junior high school staff must rest solely or even chiefly upon the payment of substantially higher salaries than now obtain in grades 7 to 9 in 8–4 schools which are similar to those included in this investigation, then this ideal staff must generally continue to be a myth unless and until the whole professional level of teaching is raised. Nevertheless, there are here and there junior high schools which have secured the services of teachers who on the whole approach the standards set up by the writers in this field. Higher salaries often accompany such a situation. But the factors which almost invariably accompany the more ideal situations are the following:

1. An organized and carefully worked out policy of selection. Too often, because of the unusual pressure at the time of reorganization, teachers plainly unfitted for junior high school service have been selected for such positions and for years have remained as liabilities in the system.

2. A rigidly enforced preparation requirement either while in the position or before employment.

3. Constant professional encouragement by supervisors, principals, and superintendents. This does not pertain to definite and inflexible rules but rather to that encouragement and inspiration which comes naturally from contact with those of high professional attainments.

4. The provision of the *means* whereby teachers may acquire the requisite background for the work.

The last, perhaps, is the most important of all factors in bringing into being an adequate staff. It is, in fact, largely a matter of creation within the system rather than a matter of procurement from the outside market, and it involves in the broadest sense much of what often has been described as in-service-training. Adequate supervision may be the chief means whereby teachers as a group may evolve into a staff of high order. However, it is only one of many possible means. For example, during the present investigation, one superintendent pointed out that whereas their efforts toward curriculum revision had resulted in nothing revolutionary in the way of new curricula, such efforts had educated the entire staff not only in the content and materials and in the teaching technique of special fields, but also in the fundamental background of junior high school education to such an extent that the staff itself had been revolutionized. Such a procedure often involves the expenditure of large sums of money and if carried on extensively might prove to be a source of substantially higher costs.

Too seldom conditions which now obtain in junior high school in-service-training give grounds for hope or optimism in the outcomes of such training. Too often the scanning of the list of topics considered in teachers' meetings in junior high schools reveals that the reorganized school has functions and purposes entirely alien to and exclusive of those considered fundamental by the leading authorities in the field. It is not impossible to find supervisors of junior high school subjects who are unfamiliar with the special purposes and peculiar functions of this new unit of education. They cannot serve as the nucleus about which to build the means to the evolution of the junior high school staff.[15]

There are two issues at present important in the general field of public school salaries and salary scheduling which may have considerable influence on junior high school instructional costs in the future. First, there is the issue of "equal pay," or the same schedule for men and women. There is now general agreement that there should be a somewhat larger proportion of men in the junior high school than now obtains in grades 7 to 9 in the traditional system. Hence, to the extent that a single salary schedule functions for both men and women this feature will not operate to cause higher costs, but to the extent that school officials act upon the belief that "desirable men will hardly be attracted in larger proportions unless salaries are larger" and "in the long run better women than men can be secured at the salaries offered" this feature may operate to cause higher instructional costs in the junior high school than in the traditional school.

The second issue pertains to the "single salary schedule," that is, to the question of paying teachers on the basis of preparation, entirely disregarding position. What effect the widespread adoption of the preparation type schedule would have on junior high school salaries as opposed to elementary salaries cannot be predicted. If better preparation were required of junior high school teachers than at present, the elementary level of preparation remaining much as it is now, then the preparation type schedule, although it makes no differentiation as to position, would have the effect of increasing the difference which now exists between elementary and junior high school salaries. If, on the other hand, there comes to be a more general recognition of the contention that elementary teachers require just as much preparation as junior or

---

[15]Sometimes the degree of unfamiliarity about the whole junior high school movement exhibited not only by those outside educational circles but also by those who are prominent in educational affairs is astonishing. The following incident was recently brought to the attention of the investigator. The people of a suburban community were divided on the issue of junior high school reorganization. A public debate was held where both sides might present their evidence. The leading exponents of the junior high school idea appealed to the president of one of America's great universities, which was located near by, believing that a letter from this well known educator might aid greatly in winning the support of the people to the reorganization movement. However, the university president pointed out in reply to this request that he was not sympathetic with the junior high school movement because he felt that boys and girls should have four years in high school instead of three. He mistakenly understood the junior high school movement to be a replacement of the four years of regular secondary education with only three years of such work. This happened, not two decades ago when the junior high school movement was still young, but less than half a decade ago.

senior high school teachers, then the use of the preparation type schedule on a large scale will tend to eliminate any differences between elementary and secondary school salaries and will therefore in like manner tend to eliminate any per pupil cost differences between the lower grades and the junior high school which are due to salary differences.

Another feature of the standard junior high school and one which must in many of its phases be closely associated with the program of studies, is that which has at various times been termed the advisory, counseling, or adjustment program. Although this feature is found to take a variety of forms, on one point there is considerable agreement, namely, that guidance "must be placed among the few most important purposes" of the junior high school.

In many instances guidance or adjustment will be found to be almost entirely a matter of the exploratory and try-out, or broadening and finding courses of the reorganized program of studies. In other cases it may be more concerned with the study of individual traits, including an analysis of the social and economic background of the individual. Koos and Kefauver have indicated the "substantial contribution of elective subjects to guidance on the junior high-school level"[16] by comparing a restricted program of studies with the enriched. The guidance work in the Washington High School of Rochester, New York, has been described[17] as consisting of two phases: first, instructional guidance which is largely associated with the program of studies, although it involves the setting aside of some definite time for this work; and, second, advisory guidance which involves individual counseling or the intensive study of the individual. Smith lists[18] seven agencies or means commonly employed in guidance, which may be grouped under three heads: guidance by means of the program of studies, by individual case studies, and by means of special periods set aside for this work. Koos,[19] although he names sixteen separate means of guidance, lists them in three groups: first, those which are curricular in nature; second, those associated with the testing and individual case study movement; and third, those associated with

[16]L. V. Koos and G. N. Kefauver, *Guidance in Secondary Schools*, pp. 54–57, The Macmillan Company, 1932.
[17]A. Laura McGregor, "A Program of Educational Guidance in the Junior High School," pp. 60–61. *Eighth Yearbook of the National Association of Secondary School Principals*, 1924.
[18]W. A. Smith, *The Junior High School*, p. 383, The Macmillan Company, 1925.
[19]L. V. Koos, *The Junior High School*, pp. 416–417.

extracurricular activities.   Dickson,[20] in describing the counseling activities of such California cities as Berkeley, Pasadena, Fresno, Los Angeles, Sacramento, and San Diego, points out that the following plans of organization, "extending from highly centralized to quite decentralized systems," are in use:

1. A centralized system with program-making adjustments and record-keeping centered in one person and one office.
2. A counseling staff, each member having a specific class or section of the school in charge.
3. Teaching counselors, each devoting a period or two daily to counseling duties.
4. The home-room or advisory teacher responsible for all adjustments of the small group of pupils assigned to that home room.

Each of these plans can, of course, overlap others by embracing elements of one or more of the others.   A combination of all four seems to the writer to be the best solution.[21]

Whatever the type of organization, or whatever the means of accomplishing a program of guidance, from a cost standpoint there are two phases to the question: first, that phase of guidance and adjustment which is so associated with the program of studies and the regular work of classroom and home-room teachers as to be more an integral part of the reorganized program of studies than a separate program of guidance; and second, that phase which involves the time of the staff in addition to classroom, home-room, or guidance periods provided in the regular program of studies.   If guidance is provided for wholly as a part of the regular program of studies (which may involve regular classroom work, or special classes in guidance and adjustment, or guidance in home rooms, but will be in every case provided for in the regular schedule), then it is obvious that in accounting for the cost of the program of studies in the reorganized school the cost of this phase of guidance and adjustment will be accounted for at the same time.   But if guidance is of such a nature as to require a counseling staff, in addition to the regular staff, for the purpose of making case studies, giving tests, and advising teachers in their work, here is a source of cost which does not fall within the scope of the regular program of studies.   The San Diego, California, situation where "our aim is to have one teacher, the home-room teacher, responsible for the

[20]In W. M. Proctor and N. Ricciardi, *The Junior High School*, pp. 178–191.
[21]*Ibid.*, p. 189.

guidance of thirty or forty pupils and her function will be to act as coördinator, guide, counselor, and friend to every boy and girl" would probably show little if any cost for guidance as such.    But in those systems where there has been built up a separate department of guidance with a director, and perhaps an assistant director, and a number of counselors, it may be found that this type of work will result in noticeably increased per pupil costs.    It seems that as long as "very different plans of organization now in operation . . . indicate that successful guidance is not inherent in the type of organization so much as in the personality and spirit of the workers" the cost implications of guidance must remain uncertain.

In those systems where guidance is made a highly centralized matter and where a special guidance staff is employed, the per pupil costs probably would not be great in communities of the size included in this investigation since the work of a very few individuals is made to extend to hundreds of boys and girls.    But this type of guidance service in small communities, unless used with considerable caution, might mean noticeably higher costs.

Still another feature of the standard junior high school which must in some of its phases be closely associated with the program of studies is that of provision for individual differences.    There is general agreement regarding the desirability of including such a feature, but little agreement about the exact form it should take. To some the recognition of individual differences means homogeneous grouping; to others it means almost any device other than homogeneous grouping.    In discussing this matter as carried out in Sacramento and Oakland, California, it has been stated that "inasmuch as one of the principal functions of the junior high school is the recognition of individual differences and the provision of work suitable for pupils of varying intelligence, it follows that proper grouping of these pupils will tend to improve the results of instruction, which is the primary function of school administration."[22]    From the discussion which follows it is evident that ability grouping is taken as the chief if not the sole means of making provision for individual differences.    In Rochester, New York, on the other hand, the question of individual differences is looked upon as a problem to be met to a considerable extent by means of varied curricula.[23]    Smith in his statement of the major purposes

[22]Proctor and Ricciardi, *op. cit.*, p. 167.
[23]Board of Education, Rochester, New York, *op. cit.*, p. 73.

of the junior high school includes among the adequate provisions for individual differences, "(a) enriched curricular and extra-curricular offerings; (b) opportunities for gradual curriculum differentiation; (c) flexibility in methods of promotion; (d) provision for varying rates of progress; and (e) vocational training for those who must leave school early."[24] This list seemingly gives very little place to ability grouping unless "provision for varying rates of progress" is interpreted as such. There are, however, many means of providing for varying rates of progress within individual classes. Koos believes that the junior high school should have recourse to the following in order to provide adequately for individual differences: "(1) the expanded differentiation of work through partially variable curricula, (2) groups moving at different rates, (3) promotion by subject, (4) permitting brighter pupils to carry more courses, and (5) supervised study."[25] Here again there is no specific mention of ability grouping although "groups moving at different rates" probably means some form of ability grouping. It is apparent, then, that ability grouping is only one form of providing for individual differences. Moreover, it is apparent from the discussion of these various features by the above writers that the program of studies is usually accepted as the chief means of making provision for variation among pupils.

From the standpoint of costs it is obvious that in so far as the program of studies is the means of providing for pupil variation, then any costs resulting from such provision must be reflected in the program of studies itself, which has already been discussed. Such other provisions as permitting brighter pupils to carry more courses, vocational training for those who must leave school early, and supervised study are usually integral parts of the program of studies or the administration thereof. The Springfield, Massachusetts, curriculum (see Table 38) illustrates provision for the latter where part of each of the hour periods devoted to academic subjects is to be devoted to supervised study. There are, however, two other types of provision which are not so intimately associated with the program of studies—ability grouping and promotion by subject.

While ability grouping may have certain direct effects upon total costs, such as expediting the passage of some pupils through school,

---

[24]Smith, *op. cit.*, p. 204.
[25]Koos, *op. cit.*, p. 50.

its effects upon per pupil costs are probably more indirect and not
of great moment.    Homogeneous grouping may, for example, require a financial outlay for a continuous testing program.    But,
more important, it may affect class-size.    As has already been
pointed out, where ability grouping is maintained more or less
rigidly in a school system, it may result in small elective classes because of the refusal to put "bright" and "dull" pupils together in
the same foreign language or art classes, for example.    A few cases
were found in the present investigation where one class might have
been sufficient, but two or more small classes in the same subject
were being carried at the same period because it was believed that
the only way to provide for varying rates of progress was by strict
ability grouping.

The other method of recognizing individual differences, the cost
of which may not be directly seen in the program of studies, has
been listed here as one of the features of the standard junior high
school, that of promotion by subject.    There is practically universal acceptance of this feature as desirable.[26]    Moreover, early
investigators report that this feature is carried out to a very considerable extent in the junior high schools.    However, the majority
of these investigations were based on questionnaires and if the
conditions found in the present study may be taken as representative of conditions in general, it is somewhat doubtful if the questionnaires revealed the true situation.    The present investigator
found that it is common for 6–3–3 systems to claim promotion by
subject when in fact closer investigation shows that such a practice
is not generally followed.    When pressed to explain exactly what
is done with a pupil who has passed all his subjects but one or two
at the end of the first semester in grade 7 or grade 8 many principals
and teachers have admitted that such pupils are passed on to the
next grade because there are no first semester classes into which
they may go in order to repeat the work failed.    If the pupil had
failed in two or more constant subjects at the end of the year it was
usually required that such pupil repeat the whole grade.    It was
found that in schools where there were no mid-year promotions it
was unusual for promotion by subject to be carried out to any appreciable extent.

Perhaps one of the most unfortunate things relative to promotion
by subject is the fact that it is so often looked upon as impossible of

[26]Koos, *op. cit.*, p. 364.    Smith, *op. cit.*, pp. 336–337.

achievement unless there are regular classes into which repeaters may go. There are, however, other devices in use such as special coaching (often supervised study periods are used for this), opportunity or special classes (several subjects directed by one teacher if the system is not large), requiring the pupil to take some other work until the work failed can be repeated the next semester, and in the case of certain elective subjects not repeating the subject at all. In connection with this last device the question has arisen as to the fairness of offering a course wherein an attempt is made to see whether or not the child is interested in the work presented, and then of failing him because he is not interested. It has been suggested that no child should be failed in broadening and finding work.[27]

Obviously where there are regular classes into which repeaters will fit, promotion by subject will not require a type of set-up which will increase per pupil costs. Likewise, the majority of the other devices which may be provided to take care of repeaters by subjects will not result in increased per pupil costs. There is, however, one device which, unless used with caution, will materially increase costs and that is the provision of special classes for repeaters. If the situation is such that these classes are reasonably large, per pupil costs will not be greatly more than in regular classes. But if special classes are provided in large numbers and there are relatively few pupils in each, the per pupil costs in these classes will be high and the average per pupil costs for the entire junior high school will be increased. It was found in the present investigation that all sorts of so-called special, opportunity, adjustment, and remedial classes were very costly, whether for pupils who spent all or for pupils who spent only part of their time in such classes.

Perhaps one of the things most essential in keeping down costs and yet making adequate provision for promotion by subject is the concentration of pupils in junior high school centers. Where pupils are concentrated it is usually possible to provide special classes for repeaters in which the enrollment will be so large as to result in per pupil costs not unreasonably high. Even in those cases where per pupil costs for repeaters appear to be high in the junior high school, these costs should be somewhat discounted;

[27]Herbert B. Bruner, *The Junior High School at Work*, p. 71, Teachers College Contributions to Education, No. 177, Bureau of Publications, Teachers College, Columbia University, 1925.

these same pupils might fail whole grades rather than subjects if
they were in a traditional system, thereby being graduated later
and raising total costs, though not per pupil costs. Where the
percentage of failures is high, this total increase in costs might be
considerable and far outweigh any increased per pupil costs due to
the promotion-by-subject plan.

A feature of the standard junior high school, the cost of which
will probably be reflected in the program of studies less than is
true of the various other features discussed above, is that of the
admission of pupils on bases of general mental, physical, and social
maturity in addition to achievement in school subject matter. If
this feature is interpreted as meaning the admission of only those
backward pupils who though retarded may take their places in
regular classes, then it is probable that this feature will not affect
per pupil costs in the junior high school. It is likely, however,
that this feature, if it is to be genuinely effective, will be interpreted
as in Berkeley, California.[28]

Through the guidance and counselling work in the Berkeley schools, nearly all
of the serious cases of over-age and low mentality found in the elementary schools
have been cared for in opportunity classes. Each term counselors and principals
in all elementary schools are requested to recommend pupils for the special opportunity class at the Burbank School. These pupils are frequently doing failing
work in third, fourth, or fifth grade, and yet are 13 years old or over. Whenever it
seems that such a pupil has received the maximum benefit possible to him in the
elementary school, he is transferred into the intermediate-school opportunity class.
For several semesters this program has been followed, with the result that we now
have very few over-age boys and girls in the elementary schools who are merely
"marking time."

When the admission of over-age pupils from the elementary
schools to the junior high schools means the organization of special
or opportunity classes, there is great likelihood that this feature will
increase the per pupil costs in the latter schools; because ordinarily
there are few pupils in each opportunity class since such pupils require more than normal individual attention. It was found in the
present investigation that in both 6-3-3 and 8-4 systems the per
pupil costs for opportunity pupils were high, usually being more
than double that of normal pupils and sometimes running up to
five or six hundred dollars per pupil. If, then, this feature should

[28]*Junior High Schools of Berkeley, California*, p. 45. United States Bureau of Education, Bulletin
No. 4, 1924.

result in a considerable increase in opportunity classes in the junior high school, it might be the source of higher per pupil costs.   However, opportunity classes are being utilized to a considerable extent in 8–4 systems as well as in 6–3–3 systems; so that this feature, while it may cause higher per pupil costs in the junior high school than in the lower grades of the same system, probably will not mean appreciably higher per pupil costs as compared with 8–4 systems.   Moreover, whereas opportunity classes may result in higher per pupil costs in grades 7 to 9 in 6–3–3 systems such classes which result from the admission feature will mean the relieving of the lower grades of the necessity for this work; hence, in so far as the system as a whole is concerned, they may not cause higher per pupil costs but merely transfer the burden from the elementary unit to the junior high school unit.   This feature illustrates the necessity of considering the costs of the reorganization movement as affecting the costs in all grades rather than as affecting the costs in grades 7 to 9 only.

Certain cost implications of eight features of the standard junior high school have been discussed above.   These features pertain to the grades included in the reorganized school, the program of studies, the staff, departmentalization, the advisory-adjustment program, provisions for individual differences, promotion by subject, and the bases of admission.   Of the eleven features listed at the beginning of this chapter as requisite to an approach to ideal junior high school education, those which pertain to buildings and equipment, methods of instruction, and collateral student activities have not been given consideration in the discussion.   The first of these three features, that pertaining to buildings and equipment, is not discussed here because it is in itself an individual problem of some magnitude and this study does not extend to any of its phases.   The remaining two features have few if any cost implications that are not directly accounted for by the features which have been treated above.

While the program of studies and the purposes of junior high school education should determine to a considerable extent the methods of instruction employed in the reorganized school, such methods as are adopted will find cost expression largely in the staff employed.   As has already been indicated, if the purposes of the junior high school demand methods of instruction which require a longer period of training for teachers or which require unusual and special abilities, then the staff which fulfills these requirements may demand higher salaries than are now paid. However, while it appears that the methods of the junior high school should be somewhat different from those of the elementary school, there seems to be little reason to believe that the former should take longer to acquire, or demand a higher type of ability than the latter.[29]

Adequate supervision, which is an effective means of controlling methods, may show a somewhat higher cost in the standard junior high school than is generally shown in the elementary schools of 8–4 systems to-day. Yet in the traditional systems of communities comparable to those included in this investigation the upper grades are usually provided with considerable, although not always the most desirable, supervision. It does not seem unlikely that a greater number of supervisors will be required in the standard reorganized school than is often provided in the traditional school.

Methods of instruction may affect the materials of instruction and thereby influence costs. There is little evidence to show that the reorganized program of studies or the changed methods of instruction will materially affect the cost of textbooks furnished. But the broadened and enriched program as well as some of the newer methods of instruction, such as the project or problem-project, do call for library facilities seldom offered by the traditional school. Likewise, they may call for various other materials of instruction not required in the unreorganized school. However, the most costly courses from the standpoint of materials, household arts and manual arts, are offered extensively in the 8–4 schools at present. While there has been some research work done and much discussion in educational literature on the subject of the standardizing and handling of supplies, until there has been more investigation of the adaptation of supplies to the specific need, the amounts or numbers required, and the like, little accurate information can be given concerning the costs of materials of instruction in the junior high school.

Collateral student activities, while often involving the collection and expenditure of considerable sums of money by the student body, need not affect costs greatly in the junior high school situation, except in so far as they affect other features. In the first

[29]W. S. Elsbree, *Teachers' Salaries*, pp. 52–58, Bureau of Publications, Teachers College, Columbia University, 1931.

place, many of the activities usually considered extracurricular in the traditional school are made a part of the regular program of studies in the junior high school, so that a measure of the cost of curricular activities in the reorganized school usually measures the cost of much of that which might be considered extracurricular in the traditional school.  In the second place, one of the chief means of assuring that collateral student activities will be adequately sponsored is a staff equipped by training and attitude to carry out such a program.  If this involves added cost, such cost must be measured in terms of the staff provided rather than in terms of the collateral student activities.  Finally, the sponsoring of those junior high school activities which do not fall within the daily or weekly schedule of work such as the school paper, debating, and the like, is carried on partly in connection with certain regular classes and to that extent requires no more staff members than would be required without such activities.  There are instances, however, where the reorganized program calls for the sponsoring of certain activities, such as athletics, which demand the services of additional staff members.  To the extent that collateral student activities require the services of higher-salaried teachers or more teachers such activities will increase per pupil costs for instruction.  Since there is a strong tendency to place within the regular schedule of the junior high school such matters as club work, and guidance and adjustment of a social and recreational nature (which may in 8–4 systems be a part of the extracurricular program), there is less reason to believe, than at first might appear, that the collateral student activities program of the junior high school as such will cost greatly more than that of the traditional school.

It is apparent that the above discussion of the cost implications of certain features of the standard junior high school is not exhaustive.  It is equally clear that it has not proved a case for or against the proposition that standard junior high school education must cost more than traditional education.  Nevertheless, it has raised enough issues to indicate that as yet it is not obvious that the progressive education of the reorganized school must inherently cost more than the more conservative education of the unreorganized school; that probably more important than the standard features, in the determination of costs, are the conditions and circumstances under which these features operate; that, for example, the community which consolidates its junior high school education may pay no more for it per pupil, even though it approaches the standard for such schools, than would be paid for traditional education of the most conservative kind.

It was stated at the beginning of this chapter that some attempt would be made to extend the discussion and conclusions, in so far as any were reached, to the twelve 6–3–3 systems included in the third phase of this investigation. This is done not for the purpose of introducing objective data to support certain contentions but rather as supplementary discussion. Perhaps the most worth-while issue to raise, regardless of the provision or lack of provision for the standard features by these twelve systems, is whether or not their present per pupil costs appear to be sufficient to provide standard junior high school education. To answer this question attention should be concentrated upon two factors, pupil-staff ratio and teachers' salaries, since these are the two major items which determine costs and the two items in which practically every feature of junior high school education finds cost expression.

It is shown in Table 36 that the average pupil-staff ratio for the twelve 6–3–3 systems is 23.0. Hence one specific question is, can all the features of the standard junior high school be provided in a situation where there are twenty-three pupils for each member of the staff? That is, is it possible to provide an adequate program of studies with the requisite constants and variables; departmentalize the work, with the desirable pupil and teacher load; provide enough special or opportunity classes for those retarded cases which are admitted from the lower grades or which develop in the junior high school; provide for individual differences by some scheme of varied progress or selection of subjects; provide largely within the regular schedule for a program of collateral student activities and for definite periods for guidance and adjustment; make provision for promotion by subject; and provide the necessary non-teaching or part-time teaching members of the staff such as the principal, librarian, special supervisors, a counselor or director of guidance, and perhaps other special members of the staff, and yet keep the pupil-staff ratio down to 23? There is no question but that this can be done, provided the class-size in both constants and variables is consistently maintained at or near a reasonable maximum. As yet a reasonable maximum has not been determined, although the tendency is toward larger classes. However, when a junior

# Standard Junior High School Costs 143

high school with an enrollment of 500 (which is less than the enrollment in the smallest of the twelve 6–3–3 systems) is taken as
an example of a reasonable concentration of pupils in one junior
high school center, if the class-size in constant subjects is kept
at approximately 35 and in variable subjects at approximately
25 (assuming that there will be one fourth as many elective classes
as constant),[30] if the pupil load measured in periods is not greater
than the teacher load, if not more than the equivalent of the full
time of one teacher is required for special or opportunity work,
if the non-teaching staff consists of one principal, one librarian,
one director of guidance or adjustment, and three supervisors,
figures show that the pupil-staff ratio will still be safely above 23.
Where the enrollment is smaller than 500 the time of non-teaching
staff members might be cut down, the librarian and guidance
director might teach part time, and the supervisors might spend
part of their time in the senior high school. However, the chief
difficulty which arises from a small enrollment is the impossibility
of offering a wide variety of electives and yet keeping the class-
size in these subjects up to a maximum. This same difficulty
often extends to constant subjects.

Reference to Table 36 will show not only that the average pupil-
staff ratio is 23 but also that the highest is only 26.9, and that the
ratio is below 25 for nine of the twelve systems. There seems little
to indicate that for the majority if for any of these twelve systems
the ratio of pupils to staff members is such that they could not
provide the standard features of the junior high school without
increased per pupil expenditures due to a lowered pupil-staff ratio.
That is, if the numbers in all classes were maintained at or near
a reasonable maximum it is likely that all the features of the
standard junior high school could be provided and yet the pupil-
staff ratio could be kept at the present level. Those systems which
do not offer a broad, rich, and varied junior high school program
of education providing for means of recognizing individual differences, guidance and adjustment, special opportunity classes,

[30]This does not assume only one fourth as many elective *subjects* offered as constant subjects. There
may be nearly as many of the former as of the latter in the eighth grade or even more of the former than
of the latter in the ninth grade as in the Springfield, Massachusetts, program of studies. However,
there often will be several sections of each of the constant subjects as compared with only one section
in many of the elective subjects. In Springfield where there are no electives in the seventh grade, four
periods per week in the eighth grade, and eight periods per week in the ninth grade, and where the total
number of periods per week per grade is twenty-five, there probably will be even less than one elective
class for every four required classes.

and similar desirable features, and yet which show the ratio of pupils to staff members to be approximately twenty-three, apparently are dissipating their expenditures on such features as small classes, unbalanced pupil and teacher load, or unnecessary non-teaching staff members. If all superintendents and principals kept constantly before them a chart showing how rapidly per pupil costs mount as pupil-staff ratio falls, there probably would be fewer small classes by far than exist to-day. Likewise, there probably would be more of a tendency to see merit in the proposition that if after adequate curriculum guidance has been provided there is not sufficient enrollment in an elective subject to bring it somewhere near a reasonable maximum, then that subject is not in demand and should not be offered.

The other major determinant of per pupil costs is the salary level. Table 37 shows that the average junior high school staff salary in the twelve 6–3–3 systems is $2,171.87. The range is considerable, running somewhat below and substantially above the mean, from $1,415.84 in Adams, Massachusetts, to $3,403.97 in White Plains, New York. Undoubtedly some of the variations exhibited here among systems are due to differences in living costs in the various communities. However, actual differences in living costs or in the standards of living expected of teachers in these various communities are not known.

This mean salary of $2,171.87 secures the services of junior high school staffs (principals, vice-principals, supervisors, and regular and special teachers) which show a mean experience of slightly over ten years and a mean training of somewhat over three years beyond high school. One method of approaching this problem is by way of the adequacy of the preparation of staff members whose services have been secured at the present salary level. That is, are ten years of experience and somewhat over three years of training above high school sufficient to produce the desirable junior high school teacher? The *time* may be sufficient, and in the case of experience probably is more than sufficient, yet the *type* of training and experience credited to many of the teachers in these twelve systems probably is inadequate. However, as with pupil-staff ratio, the question of what standard features are provided in these twelve systems is eliminated, and the question is raised whether the present salary levels are sufficient to secure the services of teachers who are adequately prepared regardless of the preparation of the present staff. The question cannot be definitely answered because, first, there is little evidence in regard to the amount of preparation necessary to produce the ideal teacher for the standard junior high school; and second, because there is too little accurate information about the present supply of teachers with specified amounts and types of training and experience. It seems clear, however, that in many instances poorly prepared teachers are at present protected from direct competition with those whose training, at least, if measured by any reasonable standard, approaches the ideal for junior high schools. It appears likely that if a somewhat longer time period for training were rigidly required but more particularly if a specific type of training were required of all junior high school teachers within the years immediately ahead, the ranks of those who failed to secure such training could readily be filled by the present actual and potential supply of well-trained aspirants. It will be objected at this point that present conditions in the supply and demand of professional services as well as that of labor in general are abnormal and that in time conditions will return to the normal in which junior high schools must pay at a higher level than elementary schools if they are going to demand a higher level of training. Such an objection seems reasonable. Regardless of logic, however, it should be recalled that the average salary paid the junior high school staff in these twelve systems, $2,171.87, is substantially higher than that paid the elementary teachers in these same systems, $1,910.76, which is true of 6–3–3 systems in general; that in each of these twelve junior high schools the present salary level not only does secure, but at previous times a lower level has secured, the services of many teachers with more than four years' training, and in the majority of these schools the training of no inconsiderable number of teachers reaches the five- and even six-year level; that the present salaries in these twelve systems secure the services of teachers whose training in many instances has been misdirected rather than limited as to amount; and that ultimately it may be necessary to take cognizance of the growing belief that the preparation of elementary teachers should be no less than, although different from, that of junior and senior high school teachers.

This mean annual salary of $2,171.87 appears to be considerably higher than the median salary paid social workers, librarians, and nurses,[31] the other services which claim the great proportion of women who enter professions. In fact, the lowest junior high school salary level in the twelve systems, $1,415.84, is approximately equal to the median salaries paid in these other professions. On the other hand, the average junior high school salary is considerably below that of the mean income in such professions as law, medicine, engineering, and architecture, which claim large numbers of men. If the profession of junior high school teacher is to compete with these other professions not only must salaries be raised but they must be drastically raised. And this is quite unlikely of accomplishment under present conditions. The issues of the teacher's salary, particularly the demand and supply of teachers, are exceedingly complex and may not be ignored by the community which would have an adequate junior high school staff.

Another important approach to such a staff, one which at present seems unduly neglected, is that of making the best of training and experience. This can be done not only by urging and requiring that teachers seek more and better training but by bringing better training to them, and also by the teachers' acquiring experience under more favorable conditions for growth than now obtain.

A study made by Floyd[32] of the University of Minnesota and correlated with the National Survey for the Education of Teachers exhibits data and reaches conclusions pertinent to the issue under consideration here. This study, which embraces only the states of the middle and far west, deals with the influences of the employing agencies of local communities, and the certifying authority of the states upon the preparation of junior high school teachers. Floyd found junior high schools inadequately staffed in spite of the fact that more than two-thirds of the teachers possessed the bachelor's degree or a more advanced degree.

The amount and type of preparation either in subject matter or in professional education which these junior high school teachers were found to possess does not indicate that the junior high schools are manned by staffs of teachers trained to cope with the problems of the institution in such fashion that the objectives of the

[31]H. F. Clark, R. N. Kutak, and M. Crobaugh, "Life Earnings in Some Occupations in the United States." Unpublished manuscript in Department of Educational Economics, Teachers College, Columbia University.

[32]Oliver R. Floyd, *The Preparation of Junior High School Teachers*, Bulletin 1932, No. 20, United States Department of the Interior.

junior high school may be achieved.   Objective evidence of the extent to which the junior high school is attaining the purposes which have been posited for it is scanty. If further investigation of this problem should indicate that the objectives are being met, something other than the specialized preparation of the teachers must be responsible for the results.

Floyd concludes that if junior high schools are to be adequately staffed the following things must be done (in addition to others):

Certification laws should recognize the need for preparation for the junior high school by providing junior high school certificates or, preferably, junior-senior (6–year) high school certificates.   Certification by subject and preparation for the guidance and extracurricular responsibilities of junior high school teachers should be characteristic of these credentials.

Teacher-training institutions must develop functional curricula for the preparation of junior high school teachers based upon the duties which this group of teachers are called upon to perform and formulated in the light of the peculiar functions of the junior high school.   These training provisions may need to take the form of in-service preparation of teachers.   Facilities should then be provided in extension courses, summer sessions, and late-afternoon classes.

Local communities should develop standards of selection which will insure the employment of teachers properly trained for the junior high school and the assignment of these teachers to programs for which they are fitted.

The use of a variety of means to insure the continued professional growth of teachers who remain in service is essential.   The teacher must be encouraged to study his problem and the administration must seek to guide this study and insure its application in the schools.   *Reliance upon the salary schedule to motivate this growth is apparently ineffective.*[33]

It is probably true that in aiming toward standardized junior high school education reorganized schools might attain their objective more readily if they could increase their expenditures somewhat.   There appear to be several other avenues of approach, however, which in the aggregate are considerably more important than expenditures.   Particularly in many of the factors which affect pupil-staff ratio much can be done to replace unnecessarily costly practices with the features of the standard junior high school without appreciably affecting costs.   Much of this depends upon the degree to which junior high school education is concentrated in larger units and upon administrative practices which affect class-size.

[33]Italics are those of the present writer.

# X
# Summary and Conclusions

THE purpose of this chapter is partly to restate, in brief form, the need of the study, its limits, and its major phases; but primarily the purpose is to state more concisely than has been done elsewhere the findings of the investigation. This latter is done, first, by summarizing the major findings and drawing certain specific conclusions therefrom, and second, by drawing more generalized conclusions, particularly as they relate to the fourth phase of the investigation.

## NEED OF THE STUDY

Because of certain a priori considerations and because of a number of investigations the junior high school as opposed to the traditional type of organization is often associated with higher costs. An examination of these investigations revealed to the writer the need for more critical study of various aspects of the problem, particularly as the problem is related to certain assumptions commonly made.

Previous investigations have generally found per pupil costs in the junior high school unit (either grades 7 and 8 or 7 to 9) higher than in the elementary unit (grades 1 to 6). Assuming that per pupil costs in grades 1 to 6 would remain the same through grades 7 and 8 in the 8–4 organization, investigators have concluded that systems with junior high schools cost more than those without. More recent investigations of the 6–3–3 type of organization have indicated that whereas such a system means increased per pupil costs in grades 7 and 8 it also means decreased costs in grade 9. This involves the further assumption that without junior high school organization per pupil costs in grades 10 to 12 would remain the same with grade 9 included. This investigation reports and examines certain aspects of the cost of junior high school education without making such assumptions.

There is the further need of the study because the majority of the previous investigations were undertaken at a time when junior high school cost data were less available and less reliable than they are to-day. This was partly due to inadequacy of financial records and reports but primarily due to the transitional nature of junior high schools until more recent times.

## LIMITS OF THE STUDY

The study is limited to costs per pupil in average daily attendance for current expense in junior high schools organized on the 6–3–3 basis in cities of 5,000 or more total population in six eastern states.

## PHASES OF THE STUDY

The study is divided into four phases. The first three phases report and examine (1) the financial support accorded grades 7 to 9 as opposed to that accorded grades K to 6 and 10 to 12 in 6–3–3 systems; (2) the per pupil costs in 6–3–3 systems as a whole compared with those in 8–4 systems; (3) the per pupil costs in grades 7 to 9 in 6–3–3 organizations as opposed to costs in these grades in 8–4 organizations. The fourth phase analyzes the cost implications of the various features of the standard junior high school.

The first three phases, although reported as differentiated aspects of the problem of junior high school costs, have a common purpose in this study, that of determining the cost effects of the 6–3–3 *type of organization* as opposed to the 8–4. In these phases no attempt is made to relate costs to the junior high school idea as expressed in a *program of education*.

The fourth phase examines the cost implications of the major features of the ideal or standard junior high school educational program with particular reference to the effect of the 6–3–3 organization upon the cost of a program of education which includes the features ordinarily associated with the junior high school idea.

## SUMMARY

1. The mean per pupil costs in one hundred seven 6–3–3 systems were found to be $96.23 in grades K to 6, $128.80 in grades 7 to

9, $162.23 in grades 10 to 12, and $114.46 in grades K to 12.   This places costs in grades 7 to 9 33.8 per cent and in 10 to 12 68.6 per cent above those in grades K to 6.   Hence the junior high school grades show an average cost approximately midway between costs in grades K to 6 and 10 to 12.   This finding is in substantial agreement with the investigation reported in Chapter VI of the *Fifth Yearbook* of the Department of Superintendence.

2.  The range of per pupil costs in grades 7 to 9 in the one hundred seven 6–3–3 systems was found to be wide, from $72.42 to $355.50.   Yet the ranges in grades K to 6 and 10 to 12 likewise were wide, from $47.67 to $287.91 and from $94.85 to $411.70 respectively.   Moreover, per pupil costs in grades 7 to 9 show a correlation of .88 with per pupil costs in grades K to 6.   This indicates a strong tendency for high elementary costs to be accompanied by high junior high school costs and for low elementary costs to be accompanied by low junior high school costs.   This finding appears not to support the belief often held that junior high school education is highly unstable and fluctuates widely from community to community with little relation to educational policy in the other administrative units.   It appears that those factors or elements which in each community determine the level of costs in grades K to 6 likewise determine to a considerable degree costs in grades 7 to 9.   A correlation of .80 was found both between grades 7 to 9 and 10 to 12 and between grades K to 6 and 10 to 12. Hence, whereas there is considerable correlation between the costs in all units of grades, the closest relationship is between the elementary and junior high school units.

3.  A comparison by states of the ratio of costs between grades 7 to 9 and K to 6 in one hundred seven 6–3–3 systems revealed that per pupil costs in the junior high school unit exceed per pupil costs in the elementary unit by 28.1 per cent in New York, 30.1 per cent in Massachusetts, 40.7 per cent in New Jersey, 45.3 per cent in Pennsylvania, 46.5 per cent in Connecticut, 61.5 per cent in Rhode Island, and 36.4 per cent in the six states.   This shows that the average financial support accorded grades 7 to 9 in comparison with that accorded grades K to 6 varies substantially from state to state.

4.  A comparison by population groups of the ratio of costs between grades 7 to 9 and K to 6 in one hundred seven 6–3–3 systems revealed that per pupil costs in the junior high school unit exceed

per pupil costs in the elementary unit by 28.8 per cent in the 10,000 to 30,000 population group, 34.5 per cent in the 5,000 to 10,000 population group, 34.7 per cent in the population group of more than 100,000, and 40.7 per cent in the 30,000 to 100,000 population group. This indicates that there are no apparent, significant cost trends between population groups, the smallest and largest groups showing almost identical variations.

5. Substantially and consistently higher per pupil costs in grades 7 to 9 than in grades K to 6 (in the one hundred seven 6–3–3 systems) do not appear to support the contention that junior high school costs so closely approximate elementary costs "as not to be reassuring as to the extent and quality of reorganization effected." That is, while higher costs are not proof of ideal or standard junior high school education, they do indicate, in so far as costs are concerned, the possibilities in grades 7 to 9 of an educational program considerably differentiated from that in the lower grades.

6. While per pupil costs in grades 7 to 9 in the 6–3–3 systems in Massachusetts were found to exceed those in grades K to 6 by 30.1 per cent, per pupil costs on the whole in the reorganized systems of that state were found to be less than in the traditional systems. The 6–3–3 and 8–4 organizations respectively showed per pupil costs of $89.69 and $92.03 in grades K to 8, $135.49 and $134.37 in grades 9 to 12, and $100.05 and $102.34 in grades K to 12.

In comparing twelve selected 6–3–3 and twelve selected 8–4 systems it was found that in the former the mean of the per pupil costs in grades 7 to 9 exceeded that in grades K to 6 by 25.1 per cent and in the latter by 24.5 per cent.

These findings show that although per pupil costs in the junior high school unit exceed per pupil costs in the elementary unit in 6–3–3 systems, the costs in these organizations as a whole are substantially the same as in 8–4 organizations, and in 6–3–3 systems costs in grades 7 to 9 bear a ratio to costs in grades K to 6 which is almost identical with the ratio in 8–4 systems.

This indicates that the cost effects of these two types of organization are such that the determination of whether or not a system shall remain 8–4 or shall shift to the 6–3–3 plan must rest upon considerations other than those of a financial nature, so far as current expense is concerned.

7. Per pupil costs were found to be higher in grades 7 to 9 than in grades K to 6 in 8–4 systems because costs in grades 7 and 8 as well as in grade 9 were materially higher than in grades K to 6. For the twelve selected 8–4 systems the mean of the per pupil costs in grades 7 and 8 exceeded that of grades K to 6 by 21.6 per cent, and in every system costs were higher in grades 7 and 8 than in the lower grades. Moreover, while it was found that the mean in grade 9 exceeded the mean in grades K to 6 by 31.0 per cent, in one half of the systems costs were higher in grades 7 and 8 than in grade 9. Furthermore, while per pupil costs in grade 9 were 31.0 per cent higher than in grades K to 6, per pupil costs in grades 10 to 12 were 63.6 per cent higher than in grades K to 6. Not only were the costs in grades 10 to 12 higher, but they were found to be materially so in every system but one.

These findings are contrary to a considerable body of opinion and indicate that in the cities studied, whereas grade 9 costs in 8–4 systems are not appreciably higher than grade 9 costs in 6-3-3 systems, neither are costs in grades 7 and 8 in 8–4 systems materially lower than in these same grades in 6–3–3 systems. Hence costs in grades 7 and 8 in 8–4 systems contribute substantially to produce costs in grades 7 to 9 which bear a ratio to costs in grades K to 6 similar to the ratio in 6–3–3 systems.

These findings indicate that it is unsound to assume either that per pupil costs in grades 7 and 8 are the same as in grades K to 6, or that per pupil costs in grade 9 are the same as in grades 10 to 12, in 8–4 systems. Therefore, it is not valid to assume that in the 8–4 type of organization the per pupil costs in the first six grades would remain the same through grades 7 and 8, and that per pupil costs in grades 10 to 12 would be the same with grade 9 included.

These findings indicate further that it would be highly desirable to improve, to make more uniform, and to extend the accounting procedure of public schools. Cost accounting should particularly make available the cost trends of various grades or units of grades.

8. Analysis of expenditures by character classification revealed that the ratios of per pupil costs between grades 7 to 9 and K to 6 show great similarity in 6–3–3 and 8–4 systems for instructional salaries, for instructional costs other than salaries, and for operation. The ratio of costs for auxiliary agencies was found to be

higher in 6–3–3 systems than in 8–4.   This appears to result from certain inherent features of the junior high school.   Such organizations tend to concentrate educational facilities in larger units which draw from greater areas.   This often requires more transportation service and greater provision for lunch-room service. Likewise, reorganized schools usually provide more athletic facilities in grades 7 to 9 than do traditional schools in grades 7 and 8.

The ratio of costs for maintenance between grades 7 to 9 and K to 6 was found to be lower in 6–3–3 systems than in 8–4.   Apparently this is because the reorganization movement is often accompanied by a building program and grades 7 to 9 in 6–3–3 systems are housed in buildings which are newer and generally require less upkeep.

The somewhat lower costs found for coördinate activities in 6–3–3 systems were partly explained by the tendency to lessen materially or to discontinue entirely medical, dental, and nursing service at the end of grade 6 in 6–3–3 systems, whereas such service is extended through grade 8 in 8–4 systems.   However, the appreciably and consistently higher per pupil costs for coordinate activities in grades K to 6 as well as in the upper grades in 8–4 systems could not be explained.

The somewhat higher ratio of costs for fixed charges between grades 7 to 9 and K to 6 in 6–3–3 systems appears to be due to variations between states in the practices affecting the payments of teachers' pensions rather than to any inherent differences between the 6–3–3 and 8–4 types of organization.

The character classification of expenditures reveals, for the major items, no significant cost trends which are inherent in the 6–3–3 type of organization.   Apparently, reorganization results in higher costs for auxiliary agencies and in lower costs for coordinate activities.   Differences for other character items appear to be due to factors not associated with type of organization.

9. It was found in the 6–3–3 systems that 78 per cent and in the 8–4 systems that 76.8 per cent of the cost differences between grades 7 to 9 and K to 6 were due to instructional salaries.   Differences in instructional salaries are accounted for by variations in salaries and in pupil-staff ratio.   The number of pupils per staff member in grades K to 6 was found to exceed that in grades 7 to 9 by 2.4 in 6–3–3 systems and by 2.5 in 8–4 systems.   The average salary paid staff members in grades 7 to 9 exceeded that paid

in grades K to 6 by $261.11 in the 6–3–3 systems and by $249.49 in the 8–4 systems. Therefore, in this investigation the variations between grades 7 to 9 and K to 6 in pupil-staff ratio and average salaries, the two major determinants of per pupil cost differences, are similar for the two types of organization.

10. In forty-seven 8–4 systems in Massachusetts it was found that the enrollment in grades 7 and 8 was such that if all classes in the lower grades were continued through grade 8 there would be only 26.6 pupils per class in the upper grades compared with 30 per class in grades 1 to 6. This decreasing enrollment coupled with the common practice, followed particularly in the smaller elementary schools, of continuing lower grade classes through grade 8, apparently accounts for much of the smaller pupil-staff ratio, and hence higher per pupil costs in grades 7 and 8.

In forty-two 6–3–3 systems in Massachusetts the ratio of enrollment in grades 7 and 8 to that in grades K to 6 is almost identical with that shown by the 8–4 systems. Yet the factor of decreasing enrollment does not operate greatly in 6–3–3 systems to lower pupil-staff ratio since it is an almost universal practice for the junior high school unit to draw pupils from more than one elementary school. That is, there is no tendency for elementary classes to retain their identity in the junior high school. Hence all classes may be started at a maximum in grade 7 in the reorganized school. Therefore, when junior high school classes are unduly small it is because advantage is not taken of this important factor inherent in the reorganized system, or because the nature of the subject demands a small class-size. On the other hand, small classes in grades 7 and 8 in traditional systems are usually due to the practice of continuing all lower grade classes through grades 7 and 8. Therefore, the tendency of junior high school organizations to bring large numbers of children together in grades 7 and 8 is an inherent factor of major importance tending toward lower per pupil costs.

11. Salaries average higher in grades 7 to 9 than in grades K to 6 in 8–4 systems, not only because of the presence of grade 9 but also because salaries in grades 7 and 8 are usually appreciably higher than in the lower grades. This is due not to a tendency to differentiate between the lower and upper grades in the salary schedule but to a tendency to place teachers with more training and more experience in the upper grades.

Salaries average higher in grades 7 to 9 than in grades K to 6 in 6–3–3 systems because usually a longer period of training is required and also because of the practice of placing junior high school teachers on a salary schedule which carries a higher base rate than that of the elementary grades.

The present investigation indicates that there is a tendency for salaries paid the staff in grades 7 to 9 to bear a ratio to salaries paid the staff in grades K to 6 which is similar in both types of organization.

12. The provision in grades 7 and 8 in 8–4 systems of certain features of progressive education which in the past have been associated only with junior high schools tends to increase costs in these two upper grades in comparison with grades 1 to 6. It is now common for 8–4 systems to offer in the upper grades certain subjects, such as the practical arts, which, as in 6–3–3 systems, appear to demand smaller classes. It likewise is common to provide such features as departmentalization, means of recognizing individual differences, and counseling and guidance. Whereas these may not operate materially to increase per pupil costs in many 6–3–3 systems since enrollment is relatively large, such features will often tend to increase costs in 8–4 systems, because in these organizations the number of pupils per grade in any one elementary school tends to be relatively small. Hence, while certain features of progressive education may tend to increase costs in the junior high school type of organization, these same features probably will be even more costly in traditional systems.

13. Costs in grade 9 were found to be substantially and consistently lower than in grades 10 to 12 in 8–4 systems because of larger class-size in grade 9 and because those teachers with less training and experience tend to spend more time in grade 9 than in grades 10 to 12.

14. No community need face the problem of reorganization unaware of its cost implications, so far as current expense is concerned. The junior high school type of organization does not automatically increase per pupil costs. Its costs will be determined by the features which it provides. And each feature may be analyzed in terms of its effects upon pupil-staff ratio and upon salaries paid, the two major determinants of per pupil cost variations.

If the program of education of the reorganized school requires fewer pupils per staff member and higher salaries, then it will cost more. Whether or not the junior high school will cost more is largely a matter of the conditions which prevail in each community. In many 8–4 systems the ratio of pupils to staff members and the salaries of staff members are such that effective junior high school education might be provided without increasing per pupil costs, and in some cases might result in lowered costs. In other 8–4 systems conditions are such that reorganization would result in increased costs.

15. An examination of the standard junior high school program of education, feature by feature, revealed that many of the factors which, by lowering pupil-staff ratio, operate to increase per pupil costs, tend to operate mostly in schools of small enrollment. Elective subjects, provision for individual differences, departmentalization, promotion by subject, and the admission of scholastically retarded pupils all tend to increase the administrative difficulties of maintaining classes at a maximum size in the small school, but need have little effect in the large. A desirable advisory-counseling-adjustment program, promotion by subject, admission of retarded pupils, an adequate system of student activities and provision for individual differences, all tend to increase the number of non-teaching staff members. The effect on pupil-staff ratio is negligible in the large school; it is much more significant in the small. Finally, the introduction of the broadened and enriched program of studies means the introduction of certain subjects which appear inherently to demand smaller classes. To the extent that such classes are introduced into 6–3–3 systems and not into 8–4 systems, the former will tend to cost more than the latter.

16. Junior high school education is often made costly because pupil load and teacher load are not identical. If this feature were inherent in the junior high school program, it would be a factor of major importance tending toward significantly higher costs in these schools as opposed to many traditional schools. That it is not inherent in reorganized education is illustrated by such 6–3–3 programs as that of Springfield, Massachusetts, where pupil load and teacher load are practically identical. Departmentalization in the upper grades of 8–4 systems often results in such a lessened teacher load that costs are materially increased.

17. Larger classes are found in many junior high schools than

in the corresponding grades in traditional schools. Yet the average class-size has increased but little because many smaller classes are found as well. Much of the lower cost which might accrue to 6-3-3 systems through lowered per pupil costs resulting from the presence of larger numbers of pupils per grade in any given school is frequently not realized in actual practice. This is due to the fact that an unnecessary number of small classes are permitted to exist.

18. This investigation revealed that the average training of junior high school teachers was well over three years. However, the type of preparation either in subject matter or in professional education does not indicate that the junior high schools are staffed by teachers trained to cope with the specialized problems of junior high school education. Many teachers in the reorganized school have had little special training for such work; few have prepared specifically for it. The paramount need is for different training rather than for more training. There is no reason to believe that this preparation would be more costly than the present type.

19. Whereas the mean training of junior high school teachers was well over three years beyond high school, many teachers had only two years and some no training beyond high school. Others were found to have four, five, and even six years of training. Often those with the least preparation received the highest salaries because of longer experience, although usually the greater part of such experience was not gained in the junior high school. In many cases the position type salary schedule has not operated to secure junior high school teachers with the desirable amount of training. Junior high school teaching as a profession will not be attractive so long as teachers with insufficient and unspecialized training compete on equal terms with those who are well prepared. It appears that the ideal junior high school staff could be secured not so much by increased salaries as by careful teacher selection, in-service-training, rigid demands for specialized preparation, constant professional encouragement, and proper certification laws.

20. Many 6-3-3 systems are not to-day providing the features of standard junior high school education. This failure is sometimes due to insufficient expenditures, but apparently it is often due, also, to dissipation of expenditures on small classes, unnecessary non-teaching staff members, improperly balanced pupil and

teacher load, and teachers who have not been prepared to function effectively with reference to the major purposes of the junior high school.

CONCLUSIONS

Certain generalizations may be drawn from the facts presented in the foregoing chapters.

1. The findings of this investigation indicate that per pupil costs in grades 7 to 9 are substantially greater than those in grades K to 6 irrespective of whether a school system is organized on the 8–4 or the 6–3–3 basis.

2. The difference between the pupil costs in grades 1 to 6 and grades 7 to 9 is approximately the same on the average in school systems organized on the 6–3–3 and the 8–4 basis.

3. The data of this study suggest that in actual practice per pupil costs for current expenses in grades 7 to 9 are approximately the same in school systems organized on the 6–3–3, or junior high school plan, as in school systems which have retained the traditional 8–4 organization.

4. The foregoing findings are not interpreted as meaning that the educational opportunities commonly associated with the junior high school idea do not cost more than education of the traditional type. It is doubtless true that it will cost more to provide an enriched program of constant and variable subjects, means of adjusting the program to individual differences, a system of student activities which is genuinely educative, an effective advisory-counseling-adjustment program, and opportunity classes for retarded cases than not to provide these opportunities. An investigation is not necessary to reach this conclusion.

When these factors are studied in actual school systems, it is found, however, that frequently many of the educational offerings commonly associated with junior high schools are provided in school systems which retain the traditional 8–4 organization. Also some school systems which have adopted the 6–3–3 organization fail to provide features associated with junior high school education. In short, the data of this study suggest that in actual practice there are no inherent factors in either the 6–3–3 or 8–4 type of organization which result in significantly different per pupil costs for current expenses.

5. The data reveal that irrespective of whether school systems

are organized on the 6–3–3 or 8–4 basis they may show very high, average, or relatively low per pupil costs.

It appears that in favored communities, many of the facilities essential to the provision of junior high school opportunities are likely to be provided, whether the organization be on the 8–4 or on the 6–3–3 basis. In less favored communities these facilities will usually be lacking regardless of type of organization.

6. When a community considers whether it shall adopt the 6–3–3 or retain the 8–4 organization, the primary issue is not one of cost. It may, according to the operation of a variety of factors, expect to have a school system of low, average, or high costs under either type of organization. The operation of these factors will result in a meager educational program of the traditional type at a relatively low per pupil cost, or in a more generous provision including many features of a real junior high school education at a higher cost, irrespective of type of organization.

7. Apparently, however, the 6–3–3 type of organization provides a situation which, if clearly recognized and intelligently administered, will probably permit the provision of educational offerings characteristic of the junior high school idea at a lower per pupil cost in the 6–3–3 than in the 8–4 organization. The cost implications of the various features of ideal junior high school education in the 6–3–3 as opposed to the 8–4 situation are best seen in their effect on pupil-staff ratio.

The broadened and enriched program of studies characteristic of the junior high school idea may tend to reduce class-size by the introduction of subjects which inherently require fewer pupils, and by the introduction of variables which are not easily controlled as to class-size. Those subjects which inherently demand fewer pupils per class operate the same in either situation, whether 6–3–3 or 8–4. On the other hand, the introduction of variables on a wide scale must inevitably reduce class-size sharply unless pupils are brought together in relatively large numbers. Enrollment in the upper grades of the average elementary school is not sufficient to permit the offering of the desirable variety of electives with economy since variables tend to divide pupils into ever smaller groups. Class-size can be better controlled in the average 6–3–3 than in the average 8–4 situation.

Provision for individual differences, promotion by subject, and the provision of special or opportunity classes may tend toward smaller class-size. Again, the tendency is greatest when enroll-ment is small and least when enrollment is large. The greater concentration of pupils in the average 6–3–3 systems makes pos-sible the offering of these features with greater economy.

Pupil load and teacher load, to which per pupil costs are par-ticularly sensitive, apparently are not affected by the features of ideal junior high school education more in the 6–3–3 than in the 8–4 systems. Many of those 6–3–3 systems which have adopted features of progressive education show pupil and teacher load to be identical. On the other hand some 8–4 systems which have departmentalized the upper grades have increased pupil load and decreased teacher load. There appears to be little reason why either type of organization inherently must show a different balance between pupil and teacher load. Once more, however, when many of the features of progressive education are offered it is sometimes easier to control the balance of pupil and teacher load in the larger units characteristic of junior high schools than in the smaller units of upper elementary grades.

Part-time or non-teaching staff members may be increased by such features as provision for individual differences, advisory-counseling-adjustment programs, and increased supervision of instruction. Whereas these features will tend to increase the number of staff members in proportion to pupils in either the 6–3–3 or 8–4 situation, they will probably have more of a tendency to do so in the latter than in the former because of the size of the unit.

Pupil-staff ratio is one outstanding factor influencing pupil costs, the other is the salary schedule maintained. There is nothing inherent in either type of organization that should make this factor higher in one than in the other. It may be questioned whether an educational program of the traditional type demands less preparation of teachers than one of the progressive type; there is nothing to indicate that when the same type of educational program is offered in the two types of organization that greater preparation of teachers is required in either.

8. While the major conclusion of this investigation is that from the standpoint of costs it makes little difference whether a school system is 6–3–3 or 8–4 in organization, it is also concluded that the former provides a situation in which the educational features characteristic of the junior high school idea may be offered at the lowest cost.